The Best M

The Best Most Useless Dress

Selected Writings of
Claudia La Rocco

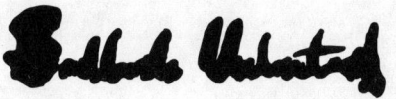

The Best Most Useless Dress: Selected Writings of Claudia La Rocco
by Claudia La Rocco

First printing

Published by:
Badlands Unlimited
P.O. Box 320310
Brooklyn, NY 11232
Tel: +1 718 788 6668
operator@badlandsunlimited.com
www.badlandsunlimited.com

Enhanced e-book with multimedia content available on Apple iBooks and
Amazon Kindles. For more information, visit www.badlandsunlimited.com

Editor and designer: Paul Chan
Consulting editor: Elizabeth Robinson
E-book designer: Ian Cheng
Copy editor: Monica Davis
Production: Micaela Durand, Matthew So

Front cover design by Badlands Unlimited
Front cover photo by Paula Lobo

Paper book distributed in the Americas by:
ARTBOOK | D.A.P. USA
155 6th Avenue, 2nd Floor
New York, NY 10013
Tel. +1 800 338-BOOK; fax: +1 212 627-9484
www.artbook.com

Paper book distributed in Europe by:
Buchhandlung Walther König
Ehrenstrasse 4
50672 Köln
http://www.buchhandlung-walther-koenig.de

Printed in the United States of America

ISBN: 978-1-936440-66-5
E-Book ISBN: 978-1-936440-67-2

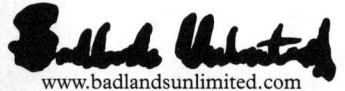

www.badlandsunlimited.com

For family, actual & adopted

I am the least difficult of men.
—Frank O'Hara

Send your additions (or subtractions)
to whom it may concern.
—Jill Johnston

CONTENTS

LIST OF ILLUSTRATIONS
All images by Claudia La Rocco

Did You Imagine It Would Be Like This?

Elizabeth Robinson

Claudia La Rocco writes that she has "argued with the obedient world." And this is true. Yet her rebelliousness takes an unexpected form, for La Rocco is interested in intimacy, and not distance, as a form of insubordination. Her writings address and invoke her friends, the arts community, and the intricacies of identity in a constantly shifting, repopulating context.

In other words, these writings speak to you. "I thought," La Rocco says, "messily of you."

Is she a critic? Yes and no. She asks questions, urgently and insistently, that are precritical. What is a self? How does a relation or a relationship create intimacy? Why does context transform any given movement or relation? Even: "Can your soul get so far behind she never catches up?" Or: "How long can a person recover before it becomes another form of not being?"

Since when did criticism become a form of metaphysics?

Underneath the definition of criticism ("the analysis and judgment of the merits and faults of a literary or artistic work") this book provides another force, something warm, pulsing, and disruptive. The linearity of conventional analysis is made more circuitous in La Rocco's works. It might even step aside from prose and become poetry. What one encounters is a curious creature wandering, sniffing, rubbing its pelt against the borders as a

1

response to "inclination, not malfunction."

So there's your metaphysics—the first principle of being is inclination: desire. And desire arrives via the question. Inquiry and seduction stroll hand in hand through these pages. Insubordinate, sexy, ravenously curious. These writings speak to

you.

★★★

For La Rocco, participating in an artwork means to pay attention and, as I said, to ask questions. She pushes against the tradition of judging merits and flaws and, instead, pays attention to herself paying attention. ("If you take notes for long enough, you/will reveal everything about yourself.") This sometimes leads to humorous reflections on such things as whether the critic should drink before viewing a performance, the boredom that eventually results from watching naked strangers, or a wicked send-up of the pompous viewer who calls a performance "Brilliant." ("It was spoken in that reverent, self-satisfied stage whisper, where it's always ambiguous as to whether the person is speaking about the art, or himself for perceiving the art.")

She titles one poem "I think we all know the assignment" with an implicit shrug and sigh. Conventional endeavors are not the kind of art under scrutiny here. With La Rocco, we can safely admit to the way our minds may wander during a dance or a poem, because she knows that even boredom can unravel into something that is startling and worthy. This is a book about art as generative error, of daring to stay wide awake, and all of the terrifying contradiction that arises when you rush headlong into art-making that brings you truly, fleetingly, to life:

"Nothing at stake.   Everything."
                     and
"this business of having a self to hold and not hold onto."

How reassuring, how glorious, really, to offer up one's closest attention and commitment and still *not know for sure* why or how the process or artwork demands that. What is it to be swept up passionately but uncomprehendingly in art without controlling its meaning? The author quotes Megan Schubert as saying, "The meaning that I do is a doing." Yes. To paraphrase La Rocco, this is the moment in which we are, all of us, unhoused. Bare (those naked strangers again!), vulnerable, fully participating.

What we learn through these texts is that attention is not merely absorptive. The best, most useful perception perceives and then interacts with what it has perceived. I am reminded of Fanny Howe's comment that "All intention reverts to attention." Such attention, deep attention, redounds once again to desire. It notes patterns of meaning and connection that others have missed. It gets up and moves towards its subject with empathy and the expectation of further connection. Attention's forms of query reach out to reconfigure the world.

★★★

Given the energy and innovation that characterize this body of work, it's useful to consider the way form, so to speak, informs it.

One who studies dance and performance, one who writes poems, knows that form itself is perception and expression. Form's intrinsic nature is responsive and precise (if we accept the poet Robert Creeley's sense that form is an extension of content). La Rocco's writing adopts the dynamism of what she perceives, and her style emerges as distinctive. I would highlight, in particular, three formal strategies that recur throughout the book: parataxis, repetition, and theft.

Parataxis places elements side by side to create juxtaposition without elaborating on connections or associations. The placement creates its own implicit motion. ("Now you see how it is a machine/of endless parts & possibilities/it can make anything, even—no, except itself.") The leap between parts generates both suspension (the reader must take the leap) and linkage (the reader finds connective tissue between the juxtaposed lines or sentences and becomes a co-creator of the text). Give this a try:

> There are just a few things on my mind
> I've lost my stamina
> For instance. I got your t-shirt all wet
> The idea seemed magical to me
> You don't call, you don't write
> You have your title
> You let your high horse slip its bridle
> The shooting range is beyond the mountain
> The leaves here are dripping
> We are gripped by the unknown
> Did you imagine it would be like this

This sometimes perilous, paratactic balancing act demonstrates what I suspect La Rocco would consider as the necessarily improvisatory nature of art-making. One can't read this passage twice and have the same experience each time. The words, apparently docile within their lines, nevertheless insist on meaning differently each time they are read. In effect, the new relations that emerge between words and phrases are akin to the "pleasures of the body moving through space," for we can recognize the parts of the body but their moving shapes defamiliarize and renew their meaning for us. Parataxis, then, may be a form of dance.

It is also a form of geography, a kind of context. After all, the site in which a dance unfolds is a defining element of the dance itself. La Rocco is deeply interested in how an artwork interacts with the world around it, and even how the ostensibly "same" piece of work will turn itself into an entirely different thing when it is transplanted to another place. One can see this played out in two pieces in this collection, one entitled "On Taste" and the other "Taste." The first, more expository, account takes place in Miami, and the environment of that locale enters into the meaning of the piece and La Rocco's discussion in important ways. The second piece, largely stripped of narrative markers, re-presents important elements of the first piece, but they occur in a new and redefining space that alters the emphases of the piece significantly.

Interesting that La Rocco would duplicate overlapping texts within a single collection, but this speaks to her preoccupation not just with juxtaposition and context, but with repetition itself:

Why do we repeat?

To emphasize or distort, to drown out the

world and make strange the banal,
to give a lie to the impossibility of perfection?

Why do we repeat? Why do we repeat?

Well, she has provided some answers for you. The turn toward repetition may be a means toward a revivifying estrangement ("some tacit reliving of foreignness") or an effort toward perfecting the process. It marks a return to a possible ideal and an immediate departure from it. ("I should miss my stop, and return, full of some new awfulness, some old pleasure.") Alas, that our stop is never the Eden that we wish for, but in La Rocco's writing, each iteration constitutes the reassurance of a possible selfhood and a remodeling of the occasion of the self-who-participates-in-and-shapes-its-environment.

Slippery self, always manifesting and then getting away. If La Rocco mourns the loss of a stable agent ("My love/ My love/I hardly remember myself") her repetitions create a rhythm of vitality and opportunity. Repetition, like the rhythm of the breath or the heartbeat, drives us onward. Repetition shapes failure every bit as much as it shapes perfection, and La Rocco revolves around those bipolar entities always attuned to the deeper cadence of opportunity. (What works? What does a failed effort tells us?)

In order to test where the self exists and whether its projects are vibrant, La Rocco does a curious thing: she steals. Along with the occasional quote, she picks up lines from various sources and repeats them; she crafts poems that sound as though she has been eavesdropping on conversations around her (or perhaps within her); she even acknowledges that she has stolen lines from others (cf. "Stealing Borrowed Lines"). She definitely steals from herself, and hence the strange recognitions that transpire when the reader has a déjà vu moment in the midst of a poem or essay. Perhaps this is why she quotes Brian Phillips as saying that we must "sustain a multiple notion of what the good and the bad can be." An idea or image or utterance wrested from one text and inserted into another forces that borrowing to remain insubordinate (that word again!) and alive to its changing net of relations. It also places pressure on the idea of authorship and, by extension, the self. In other words, the self becomes multiple, it tries on voices and masks, and "the muse always becomes something else." We can only find out who or what that might be by audaciously taking on this voice, that persona. Here is how one transposes trespass into the genius of the muse.

This too is a mode of attention, intimacy, desire.

***

Where in the end does Claudia La Rocco take us? I imagine her saying, as though it were obvious, "Nowhere." By which one understands, "Everywhere." But in closing, let me use a shorthand for that nowhere and everywhere. For in these texts there is always the urgent life surge of eros as well as frank meditations on mortality.

Every page of *The Best Most Useless Dress* finds the writing cannily "seducing this person in an abstract manner." How? By permission and intimacy the reader is invited into the imaginative project of art-making with La Rocco. She writes, "The promise of not reining someone in—how seductive." Then she claims this is a false promise, but I wonder if it is. Thoughtful ruminations on failure and disappointment also enter these pages, but the struggle to engage art fully, as a source of urgency and life is deeply erotic. If we are limited in our human efforts, then at least we can begin to create the possibility of "not reining someone [ourselves] in."

This tension, which overflows within the book, is articulated time and again:

> this is when you are alive
> this is how you spend your life
> no. go back
> learn again and forget
> & try not to be heartbroken all the time

Note how compelled La Rocco is by aging artists and their dilemmas, about mortality and what it does to artworks like dance (Of Trisha Brown's dancers she says poignantly that they are like "a mobile archive with no new material to store.") After the eros, there is grief. And through and with the grief, we go on. We turn once more to art, because "There is no medicine there is only art."

That might be restated as "There is no cure for this art thing." Its limits confront us at every turn. And yet. Art's great sexy, generative tug is irresistible, luring us to "learn again" and in that moment to be lifted over our inevitable ends, if ever-so-fleetingly: "To be mortal in the immortal moment."

Grateful that the Merce Cunningham Dance Company closed down before it became "a calcified object limping along," La Rocco celebrates one of the company's last performances as ordinary and exalted. Exactly. It's along that continuum from the mundane to the sublime that art moves, seducing us with its swerves and curves and changes.

Not reined in. Never subordinate, no. Claudia La Rocco goes ahead of us as an explorer who returns with a deliberately, provocatively incomplete map:

> I'm going into that canyon
> And you shall not know me when I return
> Not all of me
> Not yet

Elizabeth Robinson is the author of more than a dozen collections of poetry and a hybrid lyric essay, *On Ghosts*. She has been the winner of a Foundation for Contemporary Arts Grants to Artists Award, the Fence Modern Poets Prize, and the National Poetry Series and has received grants from the Fund for Poetry and the Boomerang Foundation. Robinson now co-edits Instance Press which publishes innovative contemporary poetry and is a co-editor of the literary periodical *pallaksch.pallaksch*.

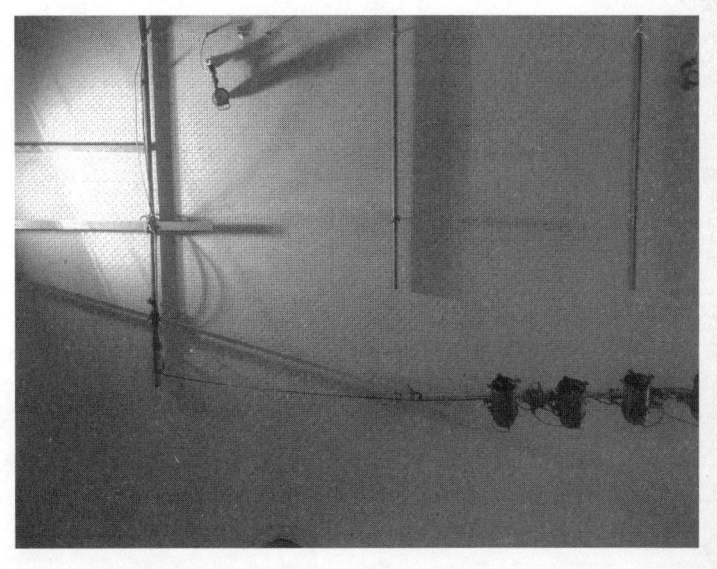

Introduction

I'm Prince Ragu
And I'm programmed to kill
Neptune　　　Triton　　　Gibbous Moon

My heart is ruined
My heaven must be learned

I need money for art supplies.

Exercise

Imagine you are someplace
Any place else
Find someone watching & seduce this person
in an abstract manner;
vectors are always sexy
Be in space
Be alone in space & then forget.

Now you see how it is a machine
of endless parts & possibilities
it can make anything even — no,
except itself

Now failure begins to please
The sun comes in weakly through the
white patterned curtains
Cars woosh by
& the machine makes a new product
(pattern)

Just go for it, go for it

It always begins with a woman.

You can tell with a guy like this. That magnetic pull.

The muse always becomes something else. Doesn't she? And then the actor moves on.

What does it mean to say you will become a writer? What does it mean to say you have become one, the future rushing up to and then passing you.

Thirty-four isn't so old. It isn't old at all. In the East Village 30 years ago, 20 years ago, all of the people in their 30s were dying. "Now I can't believe all the death I've seen," the artist David Wojnarowicz wrote in the spring of 1991. "It's so outrageous, it's like a long slow fiction that overtakes what you come to know as 'life.' It's like waking up one morning to see that the sky has disappeared and it never comes back no matter how patiently you wait."[1]

He would be dead in little more than a year. Dead at the age of 37.

People do have bad behaviors. It's true. They'd live longer if they didn't. Will this guy live a long time? You ask, is this your persona. But maybe what you mean is, am I making a persona for you.

An idea of me filtered through a societal normal, he

says. I do and I do not know what that means. I wasn't expecting him to say nostalgia is nice.

★

The young man is from Wyoming. He comes from a town of 5,000. His brothers all hunted, they still hunt. He was sensitive, he still is. Doesn't hunt. Doesn't hunt animals, anyway. Makes his way to a city with many more people than 5,000, so far away from 5,000 the number doesn't have any bearing. He remembers that first trip across the bridge, the scope and scale of it, this beautiful thing happening for the first time, this big fucking city. It is night. He is 19.

★

The idea of killing something…the bullet came so close to his head. An accident. His brother almost blew his head off. They don't talk about it. They remember it differently.

★

What happens when we take people out of their context. Some things were accurate and some weren't, he says. Yes, no, maybe, I dunno. You can't always trust the people you interview. I mean, you never should. But here's the conundrum; you also have to fall in love somehow, to create an intimacy, to let time fall away. You have to become the ideal person; you don't deny your subject.

★

Everything has a mythology.

It's snowing out, the 18-wheeler doesn't swerve, the car is spinning. Somehow you don't die.

Can you believe the actor when he talks about honesty, when he talks about not inventing the self. Things sound good when we say them, and so we keep saying them.

People go crazy for all sorts of reasons, not just divorces. It's out there. It's gonna be out there. Doesn't everyone remember the Challenger?

But I don't think it's true. I don't think everything is connected to everything else. Contamination isn't inevitable.

★

It turns out it's not very much fun. Especially when it's your own life. They all have agendas. Hard to trust them. It's a modern world. It's a modern problem. You can in fact leave Facebook. But you have to go beyond the standard deactivation. And you can't look back, you have to go for two weeks without seeking it out. It's the modern-day Orpheus myth, in reverse. You only can get rid of it by trusting it really will disappear.

★

The promise of not reining someone in—how seductive. Of course it's a false promise. You won't last on that road, not if you're built like most people. You'll fail and you'll resent the failure, resent this person who doesn't in the end need you as much as he needs an idea about himself, about art, a life of freedom. But I dunno. What the hell do I know after one lousy exchange. I also remember the city at night, those first sightings, a time when an airplane overhead meant something beyond terrorism and physical discomfort and exhausting travel. An idea about yourself and your future. Thirty-four can feel really old.

★

The young man never left the city. He wasn't complaining, it ate him alive. His child grew up, made her way to Wyoming, kept going to the West Coast. They kept in touch by letters, sometimes the telephone. She tried hunting once. She tried being a good girl.

None of this was in the film. Things get lost so easily. "Then practice losing farther, losing faster:"[2] No. you don't even have to.

★

But I think I agree with him. I don't trust her, either. That stupid asshole smile whenever he turns away from the camera. As if she already knows everything there is to know in this world. As if she could hold all your secrets on a string. And "When she was good, she was very, very good, but when she was bad, she was gorgeous."[3]

That's what being in someone else's eye will do to you.

Wish you were, wish I were
for kes

It's funny to get flowers when you're traveling
You can't keep anything

Eastern bloc skies
the right-wrong shade of orange   electric-green
                                                                        stillness

Why didn't I tell you certain things?

The hero walks in, walks out
The extras have no sense of propriety
I wonder about getting just what we desire.

The preamble at the butcher shop:
My, what big eyes you have

September

The train moves above ground
There are fireworks, the glass is cool on her cheek

Minerva tries again to be human
Her circuitry is all fouled up
Her heart is wired for an alien wisdom

Last night the clouds had moved impossibly fast
They were especially full of nothing
Or so it had seemed to M., in her drunken state.
City clouds.

Now it threatened rain
The obdurate boys next door played their games
Nothing at stake.   Everything.
A neighbor phoned to say *I've met someone. The one.*
He planned to cook her fish

M.'s cheek will not cool
It glows in the dark cabin:
This thing of being human, she thinks again,
Is too slow

Articulation Marks
for pg

This way and not that
I would tell you
The mind slipping away from itself
Well
Maybe, José (no way José) there isn't another way to do it
This isn't at all what I wanted to write

How about
The couple stood very whitely in the green field
I thought messily of you
I turned my face away from the people who might
know me

A teenager has been arrested for murder, the television
announces with solemn gratification
The people bury into devices

Maybe you would like to wake up with me
Maybe you wouldn't
Maybe I would be pleasing

Ah. No. Make it like this.
From here all of the trees are blue
You take care of the drones and when you come back I
will be perfectly ready

It is a long way
From here the roads and rivers run into each other
Rose heads upstairs, the book explains politely

The loose dirt gets all around my toes under the sandal

I wonder why the women look older
Advertising

The pretzels are no good, but we eat them
The cabin in the middle of the fragrant dark pines
stays softly
I think again of my friend's feet, how quickly they tuck
and untuck
The pleasures of the body moving through space

He says it is because he is a Scorpio
I mean he says that other people say this
A way to explain everything, all about his fortressing
People make it impossible for you to like them

My other friend says it is sometimes ok to protect
If you know you are fragile it is ok to make limits
I cannot see her eyes past the reflective lenses of her
sunglasses
Only every once in awhile a glimpse but mostly looking
at myself green-redly

The groom has the key in his pocket
That isn't a euphemism, pg.
Metal pressed into a palm
Now all the trees have more lines than can be counted
Now the safety instructions and the sky mall

I couldn't understand how the air could do that
How everything could be all lit up
And the diner could sit at the top of the hill, wreathed
in low-lying mists

Now, you insist on your possession of us
And: I let you I let you I let you

It's good that the skin could be so close
It's good that the skin should be so close

Now I place my index finger against my wrist and press lightly
The silver hook pulls against the oxblood leather strap
What some have the capacity for, others, it goes with-
out saying, do not

I said goodnight to the sailboat
I said goodnight to the moon
I wrapped the missionary around me
I only wanted something to rhyme

What you might ruin is a thing of mystery to me
But yes, I want you there at the gate, holding your smiling sign

My battery is almost out of juice
My plane keeps tilting and perhaps it does so for incli-
nation, not malfunction
Now we are at the mercy of men whose eyes we also
cannot see
I told you like this
Again, like this
Always with the wind rushing through the open glass

Forget About Your Paper Moon

The man sits inside the dubious shelter of his little cardboard shack, staring out at strangers. The strangers stare back. His body makes little twitches. The palm tree and giant swan, also cardboard, are slowly wilting, as is his roof. It has been raining, and hard, for a long time now.

The man is Francisco Camacho, and his world is *Blessed* (and also, it seems, damned). Created by Meg Stuart with Mr. Camacho and two ancillary performers, the 80-minute mostly solo work, from 2007, is being performed at New York Live Arts, where it had its North American premiere on Thursday.

Mr. Camacho is a compelling, enigmatic presence. Following him, we are plunged into a world at once particular and anonymous. The set (by Doris Dziersk), the downpour and a persistent, ominous sense that something is not right calls to mind the feel of Joan Didion's novel *The Last Thing He Wanted*, which centers on an American woman embroiled in an international conspiracy on a beleaguered tropical island.

"She liked the place empty," Ms. Didion writes. "She liked the way the shutters had started losing their slats. She liked the low clouds, the glitter on the sea, the pervasive smell of mildew and bananas."

In *Blessed* the smell is wet cardboard. Soon enough, the set has all collapsed, leaving Mr. Camacho to seek shelter as best he can among the soggy, crumpled forms. The rain continues in bursts. Jan Maertens's lighting offers hazy spotlights and harsh glares, or all but disappears to create a semi-gloom. Hahn Rowe's electronic score, though more boilerplate than his typically distinctive compositions, sets a spooky, alienated mood.

Who and what is this man meant to be? His movement, strange and stylized, shifts through varied registers. He walks in smooth, sliding steps, holding his body in semi-profile, like a figure from a frieze come almost to life. He bows down to the regally curving neck of the swan before it has sagged over, mimicking a ballet swan. Later he crawls in rapid, jerky trajectories, like a rodent seeking some morsel of sustenance.

Mr. Camacho's watchers must ferret out their sustenance too. Ms. Stuart frequently plays with the oblique and the tedious, often with thoughtful results. But at a certain point on Thursday my experience shifted from feeling caught up within the poetic vagaries of a live work to constructing, from a remove, intellectual hypotheses about it.

The catalyst for this shift might have been Mr. Camacho donning a mask with red beard and multicolored afro (the costumes are by Jean-Paul Lespagnard) and morphing into a jokey, sinister figure with slinky, sexualized movements. Much later Kotomi Nishiwaki makes an appearance as a dancer from what might have been a Las Vegas casino routine, mugging it up and prancing about as Mr. Camacho sits amid the wet ruins, his mouth pulled into a terrible, teeth-baring grimace.

You could think of cultural imperialism and of natural disasters in countries where tourism rebounds long before the victims do. (Mr. Camacho eventually gets his own dress-up moment, as Abraham Hurtado puts a series of outlandish costumes on his frame, while Mr. Camacho stands with his arms outstretched, his eyes rolling back in his head like a cross between a mystic and an imbecile.)

But nothing matches the power of Mr. Camacho's early stillness. As *Blessed* grows more involved, its meaning seems increasingly imposed from without, and its internal mysteries dim.

If you take notes for long enough, you
   will reveal everything about yourself

"I wanted to collide again."

The Horses
The Atom Colliders

Instructions for An Almost - Satifying Encounter

Stand
face your partner
he'll hoist your leg up
you'll shoot your arm up
he'll lift you parallel
your limbs will vector
he'll be on the ground & you won't know how
your knee will slide up his thigh
your calf triangles against him — ankle to knee,
   knee to chest
you'll lunge
he'll take your arm
You both will be on the ground
butt to butt, feet to feet
It's like a machine:
As you go up, they go out. It never goes quite right

They Always Ask for Water
*(with several found lines from Annie Dorsen, Iver Findlay,
and the author's previous writing)*

1.
Today was unseasonably warm
There were mountains in the distance, and disaster was
coming. I heard it on the evening news.

Dear Lover: I keep losing my nerve
Just after one week it starts already to tilt

You told me: The demands of security maybe only
secure the substitute;
Also that the soul is left behind when we fly

But who said these things first?
Already sometimes I think it is ruined between us

There is a whole pack of squid in the freezer: I will eat
them all tonight
I will watch hunting videos and read old German po-
etry, which no one understands

"Watch TV/sit on the couch/can't say much with a dick
in your mouth"

We obsess over things because they aren't true:
There are things to see & things to hear, & sometimes
you fool yourself that you're paying attention to the
right things.

Mr. Lemon tucks his thin, supple body into a white
chair onstage, just in front of a large screen, a thin sheaf

of papers on his lap and a microphone before him.
There are fires on the horizon. Just tell me I'm good.

2.

She eventually edged into view, her bare back to us,
shuddering and heaving and, finally, just before exiting
again, almost casually picking up a tambourine.

How it was, or what it was like—can the angel of his-
tory turn around?
Can your soul get so far behind she never catches up?

In the closing moments the dancers stood huddled
beneath a single caged bulb, which dimmed until they
grew invisible. Finally we saw only the light: a white
bear, fiercely glowing in its cage.

3.

I walked along the side
streets today, looking for good

fire escapes through a drifting haze
of white petals. It was

a spring party I was headed to. I
took my time. I was not

and then I
was, thinking of you. Your

pale neck, your April dresses
The expensive flower always falling from your hair

My Colombian friend told us, it's like someone said
to all the young people in the world, in order to make
good work they have to erase themselves
He blames visual art.

My Czech friend whispers in public.
He blames the Russians.

It's cold again. Why don't they ever listen to you when
you say you're going to cut loose?

Now the woman is dancing a dance she made 34 years ago.
The women watching from the friends with benefits
seats are not happy
The man is singing a song about boobies gone bad
It is mostly screaming. It is called "Booby Trap"

You're not supposed to drink before reviewing
That is to say, it's frowned upon, generally

4.

Then the mermaid turned her fishy reptile eyes on me.
"Come get your love and find out," she whispered.
She was getting pretty tired of her pink and green
kiddie pool, that much was clear. Her fancy tail had
stopped working.

The fine men were on their fine horses, streaking darkly
through the wood ringing our backyard.
The day narrowed
And the crowd returned, pressing.

The mermaid told me in my mind: stupid women are great.
It's much easier to find women who want to be stupid.
I lunged for her. I broke her delicate neck.

5.

Chief among Mr. Lemon's collaborators in recent years
has been Walter Carter, a former sharecropper born
in 1908. And there Mr. Carter was on the screen, on
his Mississippi property, clambering into a homespun

spaceship that looked as if it wouldn't get him to the market, much less the moon.

"This is Walter, my teacher," a recording of Mr. Lemon's voice informed us. "This is one of my lessons."

I'm so sorry if I hurt you. Theater is so false. One computer said to the other "My brain contains huge categories, but not one that matches your last input."

The other computer said "You are an idiot."

The first computer responded "You shut up. 'You are an idiot' isn't an argument, idiot."

None of this was making much sense to me. All of it had happened before & will happen again
At least these bodies were reclining. If you've seen one choreographed kiss, have you seen them all? I'm not that interested, but I like the view from up here

6.

We walk very slowly. He seems to want to keep stopping. And talk about politics. I do not want to talk about politics. Always the same conversation. I give noncommittal cocktail party answers. I take notes. He doesn't ask.

It feels so good to walk out into the dark city air

It's true. I lie in one of the vacant white stalls and think of the whole 1960s conversation about minimalist dance and sculpture. I think about all the things I think about when I'm supposed to be thinking only about what's on the stage. I think about how the only thing all of these dissatisfying encounters have in common is me.

It was a spring party
Her shoulders were bare.   Airplanes

came in low, their landing lights
incandescent against a purpling, yellow-green sky

The weather was holding after days of quiet rain
The neighbors were listening to baseball on the radio

The roar of the crowd: The almost-smell
of lilacs: Her thin shawl slipping

7.

I never learned to have patience for all the pronouns
in grade school we had a lesson on the proper way to
fold the *New York Times* back on itself without hitting
the paper
this was to be able to read the paper on a crowded sub-
way and not bother anyone
keep to your own space
I had no concept of space as a kid; it was all just
jammed up.

8.

You told me, you cannot get a train to Hawaii, and this
somehow seemed like the end of everything.

I have seen so many naked strangers now. If somebody
asked me what it meant to do what I do, I would say
that it means being bored by naked strangers. This
probably seems implausible to you.

Sometimes, you think you can make time go in another way.

The man on the stage asks so many questions. Does he ask too many? His answers, at some level, always seem to contain a "yes." And this was the last word he uttered. He said it as a matter of fact, an answer that was also another question. Yes. What else could he have said? Life and art go on, until they don't.

9.

Driving here, we passed 18 churches and an ostrich racing track
Sometimes only seconds in between
I change the landscapes
For you I change nothing: unchangeable
I haven't read the right books.
It's easier to watch murder in public than to watch porn, someone else told me. But I think we will watch anything, as long as that is all we're asked to do.

There was a little sign that said, "I want to be small in a big place."
I read it to myself, but really I was thinking about how you're a good influence on me
I try to tell you about communicating, and you give me a book about silence.
For instance. You never ask good questions.
And those tassels everywhere! Red and gold and tufted

After awhile I get tired of all the possibility
I'm happy for you, really I am.
Try not to be sarcastic, you say
What a thing to tell a person right before she faces the firing squad.

10.

Have you gotten more moody or less as you've gotten older? One computer asked the other

"No, I am through this. I used to be," the computer answered.

"Thank you," said the first computer. "And when did you get through it, please?"

"When I gave up," the second computer answered without pause. "Why, are you in trouble?"

"I don't think I am," the first computer said. "Thank you. But I guess I meant more, how old were you when you gave up?"

"Older than you," the second computer said.

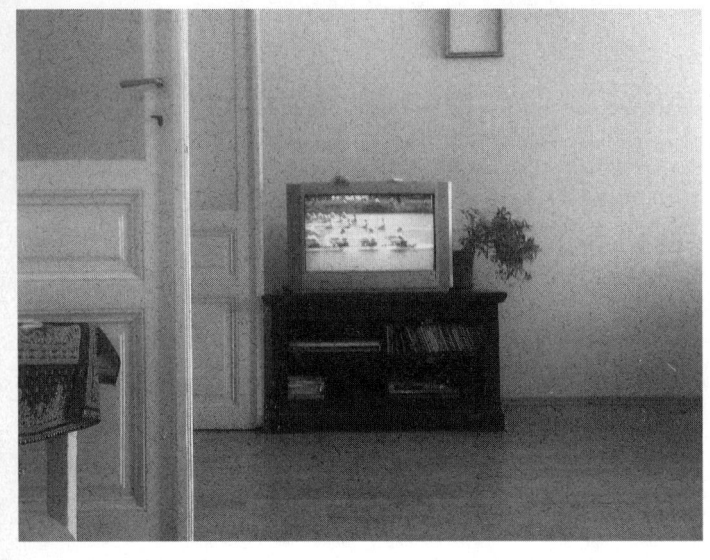

The Academy Has It In For Me

It's not enough to turn the girls into foliage these days
Everyone's interested in robots

Maybe I'll do it the quick-time way, flash my tassels
In her face

You cretins reassemble yourselves all day long
Nothing ever changes

The Immortal

Another, smaller world fell
in my lap. I put a pin

through it. I wore
it on my hat.

White Waves, Dark Cliffs

When Sarah Michelson is on, her work brooks no resistance. There is an inevitability to it, and a relentlessness, from which you do not, cannot, look away. Such a dance is *Dover Beach*, which had its American premiere this week at the Kitchen. Despite the striking architectural and design elements (created with Parker Lutz), for which Ms. Michelson is known, and a live score of cinematic intensity by Pete Drungle, the roughly 75-minute work for 11 dancers, several of them youngsters, is stringently formal and pared down.

Yet its cool surfaces thrum with simmering heat, as well as with often disturbing power dynamics and erotic undertones, particularly in one dramatically lighted section toward the end that features Greg Zucculo partnering the diminutive, terrifically spooky Allegra Herman, who is just 13 and wears an inscrutable, world-weary face, like something out of a Velázquez painting.

Dressed in a high-necked black unitard, she seems in control, yet the duet ends with Mr. Zucculo carrying her, her head thrown back, into a narrow passageway behind the black paneled back wall. What fascinates here also repels, and Ms. Michelson is masterly in mining these tensions.

Ms. Michelson has said the seeds for *Dover Beach* were planted in 2007, when she observed a community ballet class in Cardiff, Wales. (An earlier version of the dance had its debut there.) Much of the movement language is balletic but made strange, as if reconfigured by an outsider. Ms. Michelson bores into repetitive, often fiendishly difficult phrases, laced with extreme balances and arches and extensions, and often requiring the dancers to remain in relevé for long periods of time.

Almost confrontationally stone-faced while they execute grueling passages, the dancers seem yoked to a force greater than themselves. Perhaps the force is oppressive social convention; when the bewitching Non Griffiths, 12, dances, she does so with great skill, but also as a child wading into a not yet comprehensible adult world.

Or it might be the will of Ms. Michelson herself, who does not perform but appears to be rendered in Charlotte Cullinan's large green neon line portrait at the back. It is replicated later in two projections, a strange cult of self with which the artist has long flirted.

Marvelously stylized costumes by Elena Scelzi and Deanna Berg MacLean mix dance wear with street chic (hoop earrings, plunging scoop backs) and suggestions of period dress in riding habits, deconstructed formal wear and high-waisted pants. A pale yellow latticework of overlapping circles halves the stage, creating a cage of sorts on the right side, while the left is anchored by two rotating towers studded with stage lights.

These two sections seem like private and public worlds, or perhaps wild and tamed. As *Dover Beach* unfurls, the actual architecture remains, but the dance's structure grows more permeable, threatened by sweepingly tumultuous emotions. Voices whisper. We hear a recording of the Matthew Arnold poem "Dover Beach," which before was only hinted at in the sound of waves raking pebbles. A man (Oren Barnoy) in a horse's head, with bared teeth and wild, rolling eyes, emerges. And these fierce, girl-women creatures, "swept with confused alarms of struggle and flight," fight on.

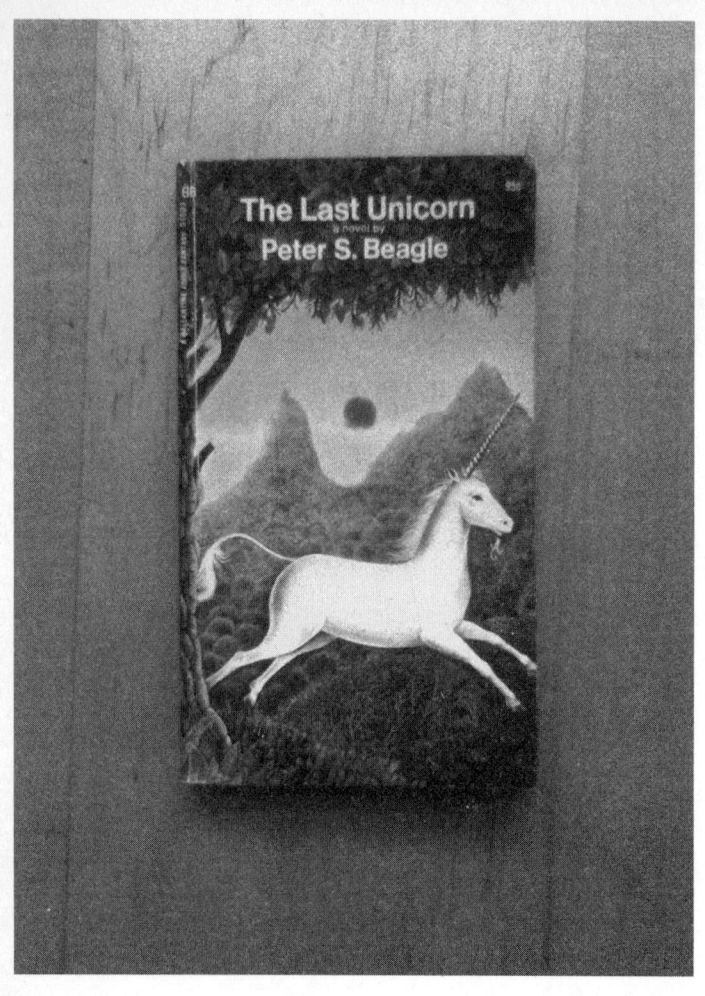

The 21st Century

1.

I have to make myself like a vole on the tundra
The leviathan awaits

There's nothing we can do about any of this

Think of a barely-there membrane
Cave beast no cave
Net game no net

The leviathan is coming
The idea of him is magical
The ice is thin
The water is black
Little feet on the tundra, quivering

You make yourself a better engine
Half horse, half function

You make a death of shivering
All the world goes quiet

The leviathan is here
The idea of it is magical
The idea of it won't quit.

2.

Knowledge of my mortality
Looms over me like a giant oyster

Pete the Lecherous Doorman is just waiting for me to make my move;
I should brain him with a sock full of pennies.

Finally, a use for pennies.

I think we all know the assignment

I'm stealing from you
I would ask if that's alright but I'm in no mood for a
firefight: same old story
You get it right.
My brain doesn't work this way
You can't just pretend to get started and then start, can you?
Math doesn't matter. Mathematics does.
Who's that boy on your laptop?
Who's that girl in the window?
It's true what they say
I don't have a mission to reshape the world, that's not
my thing
Go to the market: Everywhere
You turn, obligatory goodness. Onions and onion rings.
High up in the white room, high above the stream
Everything is as it should be
The photographer's studio—the last of the dopamine
Because I misunderstand you, I can be endlessly
generous
What do we say in the bar
After group sex?
You never told me in what way your hellbentness
manifested itself
You little heat-seeker, you
I couldn't wait, I wouldn't keep
There was that smile
I decided to send another letter to the editor
There are just a few things on my mind
I've lost my stamina
For instance. I got your t-shirt all wet
The idea seemed magical to me

You don't call, you don't write
You have your title
You let your high horse slip its bridle
The shooting range is beyond the mountain
The leaves here are dripping
We are gripped by the unknown
Did you imagine it would be like this?
The physical and intuitive selves coming together and
doing something really stupid for a really short time
The greats want ownership of their syndromes
I always think I know where you're going
And then I don't
Pull it together, girl
You're the only one I can still afford to overestimate.
I thought of a list of things to do before you die
It's typed
I'm buzzing around like a fly inside today
I can't stand it
People look so good against rivers
My palms feel so good against your thighs
I'm down to six cigarettes a day
Again. I don't like to identify as a writer
That's not true
But I'd rather watch you
Make those charcoal hearts of yours
Baby. I'll ruin you
That's not true, either
I admire anybody who dresses for dinner
I aim to please
And you. You brought plums to a household of poets
How ridiculous. How sweet
Ospreys mate for life, did you know
I think it might be my turn to go in the water
Is that the last line
Please check the archives, I never know

I see you and I think, bombshell
I see you and I think, itch
How many lives do you have left?
I want a reservation, standing please
I want that thing you do when you drop on your knees
I get all—the way a duck hydroplanes
In rapids. Swimming upstream
The way we talk about the weather
In your recurring nightmare
The one I'm inventing. The one in which I intervene
It's better not to get too comfortable
Me, I'm a contingency buyer
The night sounds are edible
I keep thinking I'll find a way to stop time
Make you mine forever, or at least until one of us gets bored
I said everything clearly
I made the right transitional statements
So, we'll see. I'll be at the other end.
Fix me
Fix my asteroid belt
I won't ask twice
Oh, but nature is a nuisance
Take my arms off
The fire burns my stick, my fingers
Your ashes singe my lips.

XII.

Pinky's been playing devil's advocate
With the local priests again. She always did

Have a way with men
In positions of authority

In her white cravat and linen suit
Stubbing out her ciggies in the potted avocado tree

　　　　　Such a spindly, miserable thing

The dark leather booth
Swallowed all three:

　　　　　Prohibition
　　　　　Theocracy
　　　　　Sin

The boys liked to promulgate. Pinky liked her gin.

Hinge and Straighten

Why do we repeat?

To emphasize or distort, to drown out the world and make strange the banal, to give a lie to the impossibility of perfection?

Why do we repeat? Why do we repeat?

Wednesday night at Performance Space 122, Heather Kravas beat the dead horse and then some in the premiere of *The Green Surround*, a dogged, discomforting and sometimes transporting sequence of tasks for nine women. There they were at the ballet barre, dutifully maneuvering their limbs and then devolving (evolving?) into erotic undulations, a gang of disaffected Wilis. There they were on all fours, "boo-hooing" in simple rhythms.

There they were, naked save for one high-heeled boot each, limping to the finish line, their rear ends forming a gorgeous line of perfectly imperfect flesh. (At other times the costumes, made by Maria Garcia, included sunglasses, black tutus and white nurse outfits). Laurie Berg, Milka Djordjevich, Cecilia Eliceche, Carolyn Hall, Lyndsey Karr, Sarah Beth Percival, Liz Santoro, Antonietta Vicario, Elizabeth Ward: these performers are beauties, and powerful.

Ms. Kravas (with fine collaborators like the composer Dana Wachs and the lighting designer Madeline Best) at once harnesses this power and subverts it, stacking often gratingly looped material so that the mind and eye are mesmerized, then worn out. "Enough!," you want to yell, as these women chant phrases till they become nonsense, count to 43 over and over, hinge and straighten again and again, exhaling as if on the edge of collapse or ecstasy.

What does it all mean? What if it doesn't mean anything at all? *The Green Surround* doesn't offer answers, and that is a consciously formal decision: here, the individual — and individual meaning—is subsumed by the mass. The Auden poem "Law Like Love" comes to mind:

And always the loud angry crowd,

Very angry and very loud,

Law is We,

And always the soft idiot softly Me.

The crowd here—and it is important that it is female— gets loud, and sometimes angry. But there is the sense that Ms. Kravas is not quite pushing as fiercely and insistently as she might. We know, after a very short while, that the name of the game will be seemingly senseless repetition, but our endurance is stretched only just to the breaking point, not past it.

If really given the chance, these nine beguiling Pied Pipers, with their red, red lips, could lead an audience astray, and beyond.

Good Fortune
for Ben, for Linnea

It was April and the rain was pouring down against the buds
Everything was new and wet
Spring: blossoms and all that jazz
I was trying to find a calm space in my head
Why do we repeat?
Why do we repeat?

Sprinkles, sugar and happiness

There you were, under the spotlight
Looking not quite the way I wanted you to look

What was it the Rolling Stones said?
I can't remember

Sometimes when I love you it feels like my chest might
cave in
I should be a sea otter
Alone with his toys at feeding time
I should miss my stop, and return, full of some new
awfulness, some old pleasure

And there you'll be in the doorframe, in that print
cotton dress

My love
My love
I hardly remember myself

There is no real medicine there is only art
How about that?
You turned sideways and you weren't even cardboard

Will you hold this for me?
The neon bull was in my pocket

The petals keep coming, in gusts, pale against the
dark trees

it's definitely like this
the wingnuts are definitely like this
it doesn't matter where the initials are

abandoning entirely
the purposely imperfect system
the secretary's secretary
it's super casual watching
retitling
red red nails
or blood
they look more delicate in real life

JO says yes - there is something comforting
about having the right fit
recent stuff or older stuff, brainwise
i have a question
can you make a machine
I'll do whatever you want me to to
that feeling when you feel like everyone's
    talking code

Anonymous

If you wait for me on the dock
Until the air gets cool

I'll bring a basket made for two

And a knife
To see if your heart is true.

Love or Money

Spring is high gala season in New York. So many parties, so many drinks, so many conversations, so many of them about money. Getting it, giving it, never having enough of it.

This quote just about sums it up: "I want you to look at this art and think about need."

That's Ain Gordon, the writer, director, and actor, speaking at the Danspace Project Gala, which he was emceeing. The art in question was static art, to be auctioned off in support of the theater. Among the works was a Marina Abramović portrait: "You could sell it tomorrow, let's think clearly people," a naked Lucy Sexton, fresh off a DANCENOISE routine later that evening, advised reluctant bidders.

But Gordon could just as easily have been talking about the moving art. There is, you may have heard, a long-standing gentleman's agreement in dance, in which the artists—the people with the very least amount of money—subsidize most everything else, including those systems that purportedly exist to serve them. Yeah, there are lots of variations on this agreement in our world—but I often think its purest expression can be found in dance.

Well. Here's another quote, from Merce Cunningham, which you also probably know, it having long since passed into Monet water lily territory: "You have to love dancing to stick to it. It gives you nothing back, no manuscripts to store away, no paintings to show on walls and maybe hang in museums, no poems to be printed and sold, nothing but that single fleeting moment when you feel alive. It is not for unsteady souls."

I have been thinking about this quote a lot these past few weeks. I thought about it when I was at the NADA fair, watching dancers perform outside (specifically out *back*), in the heat, on the pavement, for a meager audience—mostly unintentional and only vaguely interested. There was a Kickstarter campaign by organizers Cafe Dancer and Sam Gordon, announced in the press release, so the performers would receive more than "exposure." I checked out the page (which features a photo of the empty asphalt performance area) just now; ten backers, $311 pledged of $2,500 goal, 0 seconds to go. Funding Unsuccessful.

I thought about the Cunningham quote again during the Movement Research Gala, when the choreographer Ralph Lemon, in his tribute to the veteran arts advocate Sam Miller, talked about Miller having done his work "with such a brilliant, beautiful denial—that someday the boulder is not going to fall down." And while watching young dance artists working as gala waitstaff. (And by working I mean something rather murkier—as one choreographer said to me of his behind-the-scenes efforts: "This is my ticket into the show.") And when Jennifer Lacey deployed the gorgeous precision instrument that is her body, while the vocalist Megan Schubert offered a string of sentences: "The meaning that I do is a doing." "The only thing that upsets me now is narrative."

And the narrative is always the same, isn't it? The curator Cathy Edwards, another honoree that night, talked of "the time when, if you were willing to be paid nothing and work hard, you too could be the managing director of Movement Research." Is it not still that time?

I went to New York Live Arts last week to see *The Spectators*, Pam Tanowitz's austere and ravishing new dance. What even to say about the relief of encountering art like this? And of spending time in the company of a dancer like Melissa Toogood. Speed, attack, amplitude, depth—she makes the business of being alive seem possible.

"What is meant is not license, but freedom…" That's another thing Cunningham said. I found it while trolling about for the unsteady souls bit. One of the other dancers in *The Spectators* is a guy named Pierre Guilbault, who recently told me he has figured out how to survive on $1000 a month, including a room he rents for $300 in Jersey City. He's young, a beautifully buoyant and promising performer, and I wonder if his budget allows for classes, physical therapy, or health insurance. How long will $1000 a month work for him? What happens when it doesn't anymore?

It's all hopelessly romantic, in a desperate and cynical way—if there's no money now, and there was never any money then and there's not gonna be any money anytime ever, then what? Everything just for love? The margins hold the page.

Gala season. Maybe it's best to end with a few nuggets of wisdom from Karen Finley at the New Museum, offered during a self-help workshop for artists in need of money, part of the *NEA 4 in Residence* show: "When I lost my funding—and I *have* lost funding, some of you may be aware, you can Google me later—I thought I had lost everything."

"Artists—they're even more wonderful when they're dead."

"Right now. This is it, ok?"

"There's no problem. There's no problem. Everything's fine."

Stealing Borrowed Lines
for & after John Yau

I have argued with the obedient world.
Alone, while the sun bled out over the darkening trees, the

blue-black cardboard mountain cutouts. It did not
would not listen. It got

colder, and wrung the sun dry. I wasn't
crying, this isn't a letter about that, John.

I was quite calm. I argued, I would have
argued all night long. You (your

bags) were packed, your flight
imminent. You did not would not (should not)

come back. The red eyes of the airport
blinked on their towers, the sun

fell behind the dark trees, lost
in between the forgotten cardboard stacks.

Leisurely Promenade: On Richard Foreman's
Old-Fashioned Prostitutes (A True Romance)

End of play. We come to this now for comfort is that
ok? An old man with white hair I was traveling ok ok
it's not interesting being a civilian in the theater. Are
these light bulbs energy efficient? Is he from the south?
Go to Berkeley make film. Do the gals get to be people?
Do the gentlemen? This is like his apartment I was
there once and RF said *I have a bone to pick with you*
and it was terrifying and thrilling, he was lovely and
called me out for something ridiculous I'd said about
older artists, repeating themselves. But gently. Read
Said on late artistic periods, M. says. The entire after-
noon. Vermouth. Suffering quietly. Antique apertures
and argyle socks and a mirror turned on us we are
unlovely are we not?

Ok. Budapest, Shanghai, Vienna now or never. I keep
forgetting to write that lady back from *Art NE*. Shit.
Which does Samuel prefer? What if neither? No foamy
pits here. Languor and fallen soufflés. This life thing.
This word thing. Akira Kasai told me hip hop was
America's butoh. Oh my gosh. *Tennessee Williams.* Ravish-
ing. Come to the veranda. Tenn is everywhere all at once
here hurrah. Prostitutes, no. Whores, maybe. The hip
outflung. The gentle woman waiting. She is not gentle.
He needs her to be.

In another sense this is also true. Teddy bears they tie
to the grilles of their trucks. They darken and grow
strange. Susie comes looking for you. Ok. The author
maybe isn't dead, he's only preoccupied by a lady call-
er. Mistakes always profit someone. The players arrive.

No mad hatter. Alarm. Alarm. Horrible empty Sunday feeling theater tries to stop it. No. That's the first false line. "Always the soft idiot softly me." His heart is enlarged. He ties golden gloves around his neck, his physical self dissolving, he walks out into the Sunday square.

*

I busy myself with making sure the entire alphabet is there. It's harder and harder to be wide awake. Stranger an hour and four minutes of your life is over there. Plots has he laid. Rage, rage. Try to name it. If not/why not. The day lies crumpled on the hallway runner. His face is Swedish. Hole in one. No.

Then use the back entrance. No.

Lines & scarves & old-fashioned loves. It is a desperate business, this business of having a self to hold and not hold onto. Hold it. I thought this at least. I thought it. A strong drink. A mutual subject. The no hero in his best dressed whites. The whore's friend giggles. Ok. Time is up. Joan Didion can no longer wear her four-inch red sandal heels. It's often difficult. The classes are held in the back room. If you don't pass, you fail. The observer changes the observed. The alphabet—and then some—returns. Gently, of course. The enlarged heart bursts. Rivulets of blood in the gutter. No, false again. Count again the things one might do. This and that. Famous people. Busyness. Alarms. The hotel room alone late at night.

Waiting again. The beautiful coquette. There's nothing special about you. The master of ceremonies awaits. He had to return to tell you this. The band is warming up. OP EN AL LN. Rainer Thompson. Now no one can.

Look. Now there is nothing to see again. Joe Persek.
The office worker will one day be a star. Hello Hello.
The world hangs up on you the jeweled fingers slip
around your wrist no one cannot say it say it the ribbons
hang limply from the sky Beckett it isn't falling yet.

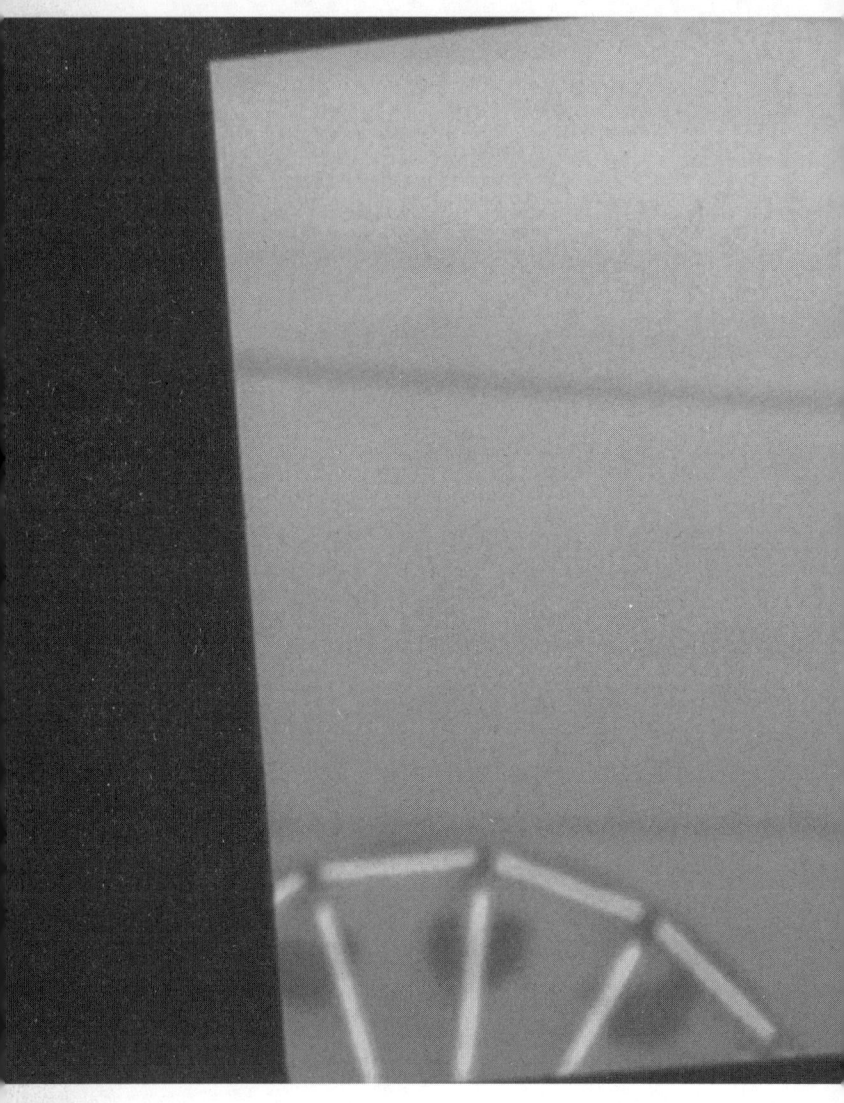

173–177 [or: Facebook Is Inescapable]

You have to climb the big hill each morning, José.
Not Said, but that other guy on your table:

Therefore, be ye lanterns unto yourselves

Maybe the self has no true home
Maybe no more than effort is ok

We are all of us unhoused
In other words, as my friend said, if I can eat good
Mexican food I can tolerate
The world being shit
Hmm.
I like this wine.

Dear Lost Shadows:
Maybe all criticism is about grief
The not matching.

But back to this hill
It's good as a cure for fog
That pressure between your lovely eyes

Zia! Here we are again
If I'm losing the woman who has loved me
Is that not exile of a sort?

You see: it's easy to be maudlin on a wet Tuesday
afternoon
Not enough movement
Or: everything you watch requires translation

Ah, the nostalgia for utopian rhetoric
Last night he held me in his arms for hours
If only I had been there at the time

No, that's not true
I'm moving too far afield

The poets killed him:
How disgustingly romantic, José

That's not what I came here to tell you
I am armed only with a ration card
& miserable loneliness
Finds its modest refuge

Oh, extravagance!
Everywhere, except when you need it
Hegel: you see, he can't help himself, José

You and your lovely little arrows
They cannot be
I don't think really he wants to talk about the masses
No one, in the end, ever does.

Metal
for LF

The tall trees are rain-dark, leaves plastered in yellow squares
like tracing paper

My love
I keep finding out the answers

I pick up my checks
I try to stay in the moment

The imperial cafeteria is full again
long banquets impossibly red and tasseled

The trap door is open, Linda
I am trying to fall through

Everyday People

"Brilliant," the man behind me at the Kitchen exhaled, to himself and his date and anybody else within earshot on this particular Sunday afternoon, during the final performance of Claude Wampler's *N'a pas un gramme de charisme* (Not an ounce of charisma).

It was spoken in that reverent, self-satisfied stage whisper, where it's always ambiguous as to whether the person is speaking about the art, or himself for perceiving the art, or some combination of the two. And lo. Just then the woman onstage—well, technically on the risers where the audience typically sits but which in this case formed the stage, with the audience sitting on the literal stage—collapsed awkwardly backward in an inflated poof of shiny fabric.

Why do we go to the theater? What keeps us coming back to church? I thought about this vague question a lot this past weekend, a weekend over the course of which I spent thirteen full hours in the theater: one at Wampler; two watching the Trisha Brown Dance Company at the Brooklyn Academy of Music; and ten (in a row) at the Public Theater, for the Soho Rep. production of Nature Theater of Oklahoma's *Life and Times: Episodes 1–4*.

That's a lot of hours watching other people's lives. Maybe it's not so bad if it makes us feel something—even self-satisfied. Or maybe it is: "I think audiences really want somebody to entertain them and make them feel special," Wampler mentioned in an interview, reaffirming that she's trying to "refuse this demand."

This is a predictably condescending thing to say. But more to the point, where's the refusal? *N'a pas un gramme de charisme*, which is (wink wink) all about charisma, is a frothy, disaffected art-world spectacle, populated by John Tremblay's colorful chunky *Flintstone*-esque objects and camera-ready dancers (including, creepily but not nearly creepily enough, Wampler's eight-year-old daughter) and presided over by Mitch Margold's organ music. There's a bored and sometimes charmingly awkward seduction at play. Everything is pretty serious, even the awkwardness, and despite the funky sound, the only people who look like they are having sustained fun are the black dancers seen on grainy, 1970s-looking recorded footage. In her 1981 essay "A Criticism of Outrage," Jill Johnston remembered an event in 1952 in North Carolina, "where hundreds of black people danced freely to a disco band and refracted light displays. We whites were stamped on the backs of our hands with infrared numbers and herded to a balcony where we were allowed to watch."

It's all a little queasy-making. (But then, not nearly queasy-making enough.) So were the Katz's Deli hotdogs served during our cafeteria-style dinner break in *Life and Times*. They were oddly satisfying (though not as satisfying as the pb&j sandwiches the audience got at Nature Theater's *No Dice* from 2007). And here I want to start inserting "like" and "um" and "you know" into my sentences, because this is a huge and happy part of the point of the company's productions, which feature unedited phone-conversation scripts.

In this case the conversations were with one gal, Kristin Worrall, who performs with the company and who grew up in white middle-class New England suburbia. We get to hear all about it: the crushes, the fuzzy childhood memories, the humiliations and the triumphs and the brushes with less sheltered lives. Devastating social hierarchies. "Gay" as a playground catchall insult.

"Did it get stupider? Did we get bored with it? Maybe they got bored with it?" a friend mused after it was all over, as we hustled out into snowy, midnight SoHo. I dunno. But I found myself a little too entertained, and turned off by Worrall's continual references to people's looks and lack of intelligence. Put a recorder on anyone for eight hours and it doesn't stay pretty. Or eight seconds—Björk was at the Public that Saturday, along with a hefty chunk of the performance-world intelligentsia, and during our dessert break (brownies disappointingly free of additives) we watched an influential curator snapping a covert picture of her with his iPhone. Life and Times!

I don't know if we want art to make us feel special. Somehow I think it's more about movement—to catch us up in something urgent, no matter if it's the urgency of the mundane everyday, something we have to say "yes" or "no" to. I adore Nature Theater for its dogged insistence on that everyday, stylized just beyond an inch of its life. But the zipping between pathos and slyness wears me out. There are more "states" than California and New York.

There's New Jersey, for example. And *Newark (Niweweorce)*, Trisha Brown's gorgeous anvil of a dance; to see the cast emerge exhausted and triumphant from its unrelenting geometries at the Brooklyn Academy of Music on Friday night was pretty grand. Some of them probably weren't born yet when Brown made the dance, in 1987, when she and Donald Judd somehow dreamed up the idea of sending her valiant phrases cutting across a stage while his vibrant color scrims descended periodically like guillotines. And now they're all that remains: a mobile archive with no new material to store. Brown, who has been in ill health for years, wasn't in the theater, and her company faces that unsolvable dilemma of how to move forward now that she no longer is.

Brown's radical days are long behind her, and so it's doubtful her supporting staff will make the radical decision to fold up the tents for good. What's the right move here? Just like always in church, there's no one qualified to say.

this music is humble
I will always disappoint you
mostly, you won't notice
the camp for me is unnecessary throat-
cleaning

this is it, this is the poem

this is the irony

yes I know you said irony

kneel . . .

there's something sovereign about Jo — but
gentle — the vulnerable regent

all these little steps I make for you

these earthly remnants

. Jeffrey does the tennis serve

again & again damming down. & then
it isn't anymore a game

No it never is . do nothing
the horns are mournful

74

Space//Space Stream of Consciousness
after Banana Bag & Bodice

It's an emergency sandwich.

How often? Every time.

He has a tiny little tail. It's ridiculous.

We just have to sit there. Yeah, that's about it.

Should we be drunk? You gave us beer.

I am drunk.

I do not drink beer.

A poor man's *Enterprise*.

Like, destitute.

Like, not going *anywhere*.

Their hands look small.

I am thinking of so many other things.

But wait. But Earth's Greatest Hits.

Paul Lazar keeps laughing.

I keep forgetting to watch.

The critic makes the movements critics make—I have
made those movements.

What do you get when you cross a fox and a duck?

Why the long face?

Zippers. Drop crotches.

Don't sing.

Move your hips.

Don't sing.

No no.

Yesssss.

Wait, what?

Maybe—oh. Her tail is bigger.

These lights are like roller rink lights (Guns N' Roses. Poison. Acid-washed jeans.)

Everybody misremembers. It's the job.

Flaubert? Oh, wait. Edith Piaf.

"Her tail is longer than his tail." "That's your lede."

Misogyny & stand-up comedy.

The second-to-last frontier.

I went somewhere else for a second.

I'm back. But not without regrets.

Botanica.

The boy can do it, not the girl.

Life was easier before art turned me into a feminist.

I'm dying up here.

You're dying down there.

Hetero blah blah.

What if I were 100 percent sober? 90?

There's only *one* bearded lady in this town and it ain't you.

★

Oh.

Wait wait is she actually in control and you're missing the whole point?

It's so beautiful.

Not me, not you.

Oh, shit. It's an after school special.

He insists.

She plays every trump card. It gets less interesting.

(or maybe that's me)

Every day is an emergency. Duh.

Oh, boobs.

He didn't finish his sandwich.

Face plant. Black death.

No nostalgia, not when you've come this far.

Oh boy.

Clenched jaw blah-blah.

Skinny blue limbs. Death.

Somebody already told her twice.

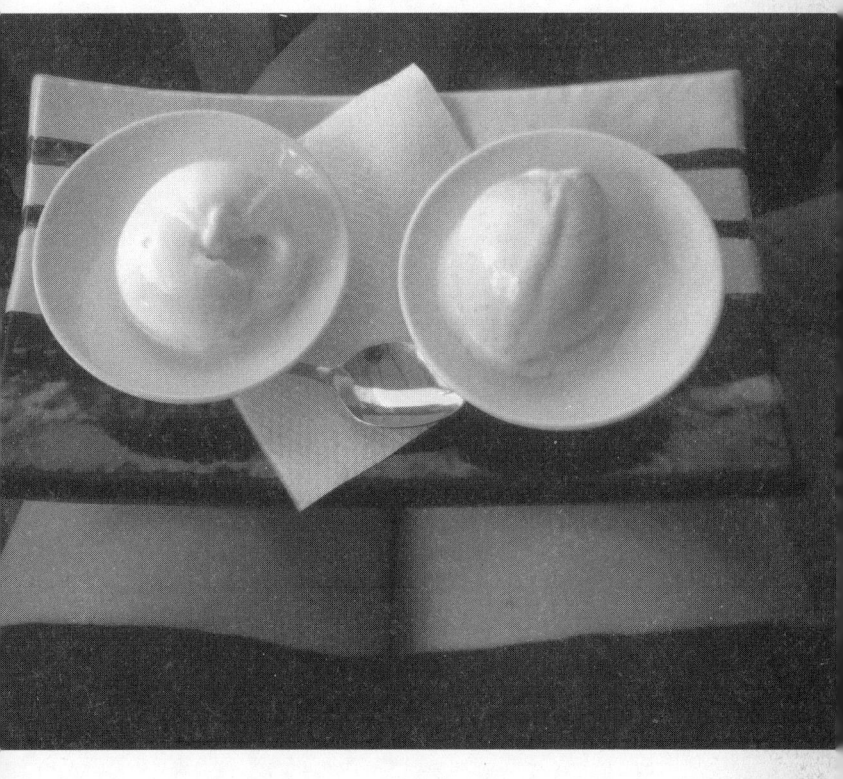

IX.

Pinky had gone to see Einstein
Moomjy about the Medallion Account. Twice

This month he'd made her wait and Pinky wouldn't wait
Again, she

Wouldn't wait once for almost anyone
Out to Jackson Heights from the St. Moritz. It

Was always something
Like this, some tacit reliving of foreignness

They had met in Kabul. She
Was chatting up the Mujahideen, he

Was assessing the mercantile scene. They
Dined on colorful rugs, ate plums and sipped milky tea

He was never one
To pull up his socks in public, he always won

At the stock market
"Very clever, these Chinese," he murmured over my
hand when Pinky brought him round

He stood very tall, and very straight
He wore an unremarkable face.

On Taste

The carpet is impossibly white
The tower is a double crescent
There is a way in which the translator must love failure
The thin line of light splitting the morning sky

Silas and Rashaun asked me to be in this project with them and Davison. I wasn't sure what to expect.

"Claudia: We feel that it is important for us to deal with our identities as performers/collaborators/lovers in this piece. It's not about making our relationship a public issue per se, but it would be inauthentic to overlook this aspect as it relates to the duet form. Certainly our perceived identities come into play. Since you know us as individuals and collaborators very intimately we think that you and your writing could be very helpful in fleshing out this content. Also your identity as a critic-turned-performer needs to be dealt with if you are to continue as a collaborator beyond Miami. We propose a text or a series of texts that act as a sort of intervention or commentary or critical description. It may even be interesting to compare and contrast our bodies/movements as they relate to taste. We may even want to repeat the same section of movement exactly, with and without commentary. The other component is that we will probably need to change clothes, so the text can act as intermission or palate cleanser to the dancing. I think we both feel that text as a simultaneous but indirect component (as in *Nox*) is not the way we want to go with this. Also as much as we love the sci-fi idea, we think it may be a completely other piece, which we are happy to entertain and pursue at some point. You of course, can cleverly weave that in if it feels right to you."[1]

And I'm not really sure what to write now, from this fuzzy in-between vantage point of participant-observer.

★

BFI is in a warren-like, artist-run building on NE 11th street in Downtown Miami. Here are a few things you can see from the sidewalk: the color-saturated façade, its rich blooms of color marked here and there by delicate graffiti commentary; an exotic dancers club; various high-rises, some of them attended to by the city's ubiquitous construction cranes; mostly empty parking lots, the asphalt fighting a losing battle with vegetation; a lot of down-and-out people, some of them apparently homeless, some of them apparently in the throes of addiction; big, gorgeous sky.

S. & R. chose BFI during an earlier site visit. The four of us (joined for a few days by the costume designer James Kidd) spent a week there in March, trying to figure out how the philosophical (hypothetical?) ideas undergirding *Taste* might be put into practice.

"The piece has many ever-changing ideas, some of which have been discussed to varying degrees with all of you. It is still a conversation around bad and good taste, and the racial, cultural, class issues that inform taste. We are still interested in the food/wine tasting phenomenon as a demonstrative device. The piece is also about a response to space. It does not exist in a conceptual vacuum, but rather its identity is formed by the context of the space. Also it is more broadly about us as objectified performers and the fetishization of dancers. We have used seventeenth-century baroque music and silence and are still interested in those."[2]

Shortly after arriving in Miami we drove to BFI. Almost immediately after we exited the rental car, a Chrysler 200, a man approached—one of those indeterminate approaches, in which you are pretty sure but can't quite tell if this is someone asking for money. He wanted to shake hands. We didn't want to. "Don't worry, man, the black won't rub off on you," he told R. This was an interesting choice, perhaps pointed, as R. is the only one of us who is not white.[3]

Yes, he wanted money. "You people come down here, you don't contribute anything." Menacing in a strangely friendly way. He subsequently called R. a sissy.

★

Look. Apollo and Dionysus. The whole thing. Sweat & glitter & spandex.

★

There are lots of ideas about dancers (even as dance, in this country, is an invisible art form, surrounded by an impressive cultural illiteracy). One of them, maybe the most prevalent, is the sexualized dancer: the knowing smiles around dancers in bed. All of that flexibility. The splits.
This is obviously irksome to lots of dancers. I'm sure I would be irked. I'm pretty sure.

Rundown on poets: precious & cloistered.

Critics: can't drive the car, generally fat & bitter & loathsome.

★

But of course their relationship is a public issue. It's a handy little journalistic hook.

84

In the essay "Poetry and the Problem of Taste," Brian Phillips writes that taste is "a vital kind of negative capability—the capability within an audience that allows it to combine the subjective and the objective in a single aesthetic experience, and thus not only to distinguish between the good and the bad in aesthetics, but to sustain a multiple notion of what the good and the bad can be. This is an ability of critical importance in our effort to develop a complete relationship to a given form of art, which is why, when we think of taste in a broad sense, we think of what it makes possible, and not what it forbids. Its very contradictoriness contains propulsive cross-currents, like the cave of winds in Virgil."

I mean it's not always easy to look
This is my job and I can tell you it's not always easy
I mean, I never give money to the homeless
I'm not that kind of humanitarian
I just like it when you do that
I like it when you do it just like that

The body works it out
The body gets closer
Standing in the sun squinting
Of course we're all mourning for ourselves
Of course we get uncomfortable around our kind
It's subjective

★

One of the things I did not anticipate doing was reading David Hume's essay, "Of the Standard of Taste," through a rented bullhorn and changing into cutoffs, bathing suit, and wedges while being driven around and around the block in a Mercedes-Benz E-Class by D., himself made rather conspicuous by the donning of a pink lace ski mask of sorts, as S. and R. improvised various movement phrases in the parking lot across the street from the BFI, watched by audience members through the raised loading-dock gate and whoever else was passing by.

"What is the value, the allure of this thing we do? I feel really sensitive to the way I was raised, the education I've had. I always feel inadequate. I think a lot about workmanship and work ethic in dance, that working-class ethic. And then something more privileged."[4]

Those people come down here, they don't contribute anything
They talk about the quality of the light
The all new & improved
Don't worry, the black won't
These two are real professionals.
They're very flexible.
Something about that white flower, that dark hair

I saw my first hooker in Miami[5]
Stick insect orange street lights stretch
It's like they say, you only know what gunshots sound like after you hear one
They don't look like anything else

★

The amount of labor that goes into a dance is astounding. So much of it is handmade, improvised, provisional.

There is the repetitive, often tedious work of creating and then refining gestures, steps, phrases, etc.—hours and hours in the studio, worrying at what will in the end be mere seconds of movement. This process happens whether the end result will be improvised, set, or something in between.

In writing this happens, too. The hours spent staring at a blank page or screen, striking through words or doubling back, puttering around the house like a maniac in your pajamas. Staring out the window, at the ceiling, at godforsaken social media sites.

But in writing you at least have drafts.[6] Physical drafts. Something to which you can return.

And there is the logistical work, when the practical realities of what and how swing to the fore. D. is a wizard at navigating all of this. It's pretty exciting just watching him work. He makes you feel marvelously taken care of. There are these big flashes of anger that come up, thunderstorm-like, obscuring his demeanor. Build-up, obscenities, calm.

And watching S. & R.—that is also exciting. The intelligence that these two artists carry in their bodies—it is a privilege to be in conversation with that intelligence. And it is fascinating to watch them negotiate their tangled layers of collaboration: where they push, where they give in, the moments when either of these things is more about their relationship outside of the studio than inside. You can't die on every hill.

It should go without saying that no one ever gets paid enough to do this. That the practitioners—particularly the dancers—subsidize the whole crummy system, often at the cost of their credit ratings. Commissions, ticket sales, grants, blah blah blah—none of it adds up to much.

*

During the dress rehearsal it poured and poured. Beautiful. Water and sweat streaming over S. and R., as they moved from outfit to outfit, ending eventually in almost nothing, dirty rivulets snaking down their skin. The Hume essay rumpled and bleeding. They ended splayed, bodies interlocking on the dirty concrete floor

87

of the loading dock. We had no more cardboard signs to hold up. D. handed me the champagne bottle, which I dutifully swigged, and then poured. R. curled his back, as if protectively. S. arched up, fish in a fountain. These two are perfect. Their bodies are wrecked; they are doing that for us.

We come down here, we don't contribute anything
We talk about the quality of the light

Isn't that something
Cherry Coke remarkable
Isn't that…

You make sense without words
The frigate birds wheel high above, sharpening their knives
I do not want to spend my life without knowing anything else
We look at war
We look at the crushed flowers from the night before
The carpet is impossibly white
The tower is a double crescent
Rubber doll, techno something
You've never met more awkward rock stars
There is a way in which the translator must love failure
The thin line of light splitting the morning sky

Florida
for JB

Me, I don't get furious anymore:
I'm too run-down
Let's all get naked and lie down, I told them
(You know, you can't say things like that in the class-
room. It's a very literal place.)

Maybe that's why we broke up:
I didn't have the right messaging plan
I don't like to be walked on

Love is a bad deal
It interferes with travel plans

      They're all kind of fudgy if you ask me, even science
                  I like to go swimming
If you're in the middle of the pool, you can't just jump out

            I was with this girl for almost nine years
                I used to be the dance groupie
                        She was ok

            Anyhow, those were my younger days
                  Those were the '70s

Then of course I made the large mistake of marrying a
                        dance therapist
        Which has jack shit to do with dancing
            It had to do with manipulation
                And still does

When I was a kid the *New York Times* was so big you

89

                         could use it for a bed sheet
                            In fact, I think we did

                    Anyway, let me know your dates
                            And let the guy go
           You're cute, you're young, you're intelligent
                        I don't know what to say
               There's no easy way out of the game
           Buy a ticket and go to the theater in Paris
                                    Why not.
                        What are you waiting for.

It doesn't matter. I'm ok. I'm in the bathtub, you're
calling. Boy oh boy.

I'll see you in the morning, poolside
I'll be on that bicycle that doesn't go anywhere
Young people. I'm telling you
You're full, you think there's no hunger

Romeo, Juliet, blah blah blah
All those lovers twisting in the wind tunnel

Membership has its privileges. You know.
Life's happiest moments are about time.
You're gonna go through the roof in a few years.
Guarantee it.
Me too.

'You've gonna get felt up a little here. just enjoy it''①

what is it always to be the outside
    the watcher
the margin holds the page

this is the key of god
he turns you in the lock

I relate to Jo's quietness.

Jeffrey & Karen always have a line ready

→ TRIO
this is really voluptuous
    sweepy & spiralling & cyclicly
the way nature advances
    & then points of stillness

the thing you keep doing
Jo's face as ladies crotch—brush his head —
    the indignities never end

always Miguel waiting, perfectly posed
[all morning I keep thinking of my dollhouse].

the foot paces, brushes back & knee hinges
    up — the horse waiting, restless
K's face — that smile, sun through clouds

91

Now I am just waiting

1.

It is pleasing you that is the thing
Ohhh the limits of texting
The wind blows the fountain all over the girls from
Hoboken
Another field trip ruined
Who knows why they have come?
I do

Feel beautiful, idiot
If the weather can do it, you can, too.

2.

They disappeared me

Even when you threw a tortilla chip at my head and
swore your allegiance elsewhere
Even then I loved you

Are you invisible?
I gave you my cut sequin heart in the hope you might
leave

I had such aspirations
Oh, Edith! XXX
Come away with me to karaoke
I'll sing that song over and over & you'll forget how to
remember me

Those are the rules
We'll be the Jackson Five. Minus three.

The Confession

The sky was falling
These things happen slow
My fat Russian lover was eating blini in the park

He has no sense of himself.
It was bitterly cold and I felt so…understimulated
I took off my mask. There was nothing underneath

My fat Russian lover tells me I have abandoned the
world in favor of self-indulgence
I nail a cross to his head most nights, hammer the hole
deep as it will go
I don't mind

The ash trees are black in this cold wet
Their dismal yellow leaves are the last to fall
They have an unrealistic sense of themselves, maybe

It gets to be a bother
I put on the tallest black heels I could find for this job
Still, nothing changes in my wood-paneled heart

There is an art to leaving your country
Mine is forever rushing into modernism
Poor feudal darling. It explains, in part, the basement
full of bodies

I gave my fat Russian lover a head start
He cut a terrible arc through the snow-laced fields
I filed my tips. Kept my scope on his floundering hips

Ponderous baby
Full of unrealistic hopes
My city collapses to its very rim

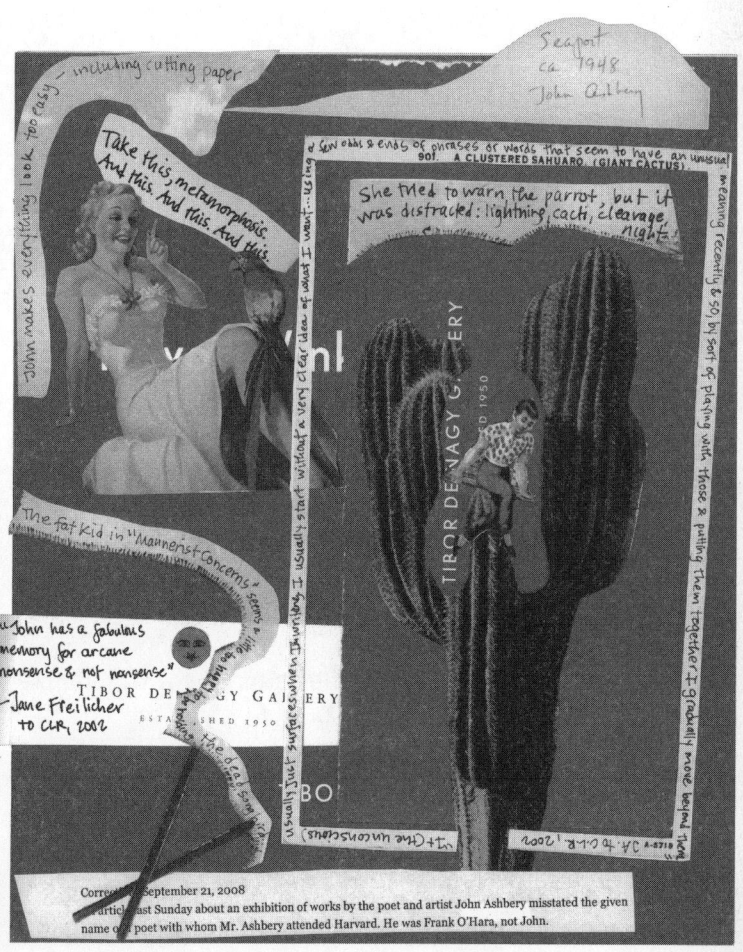

Seapot
ca. 1948
John Ashbery

— including cutting paper

John makes everything look too easy

Take this, metamorphosis. And this. And this. And this.

ebb and ends of phrases of words that seem to have an unusual
901. A CLUSTERED SAHUARO (GIANT CACTUS).

She tried to warn the parrot, but it was distracted: lightning, cacti, cleavage, night!

meaning recently & so, by sort of playing with those & putting them together + gradually more & more there

The fat kid in "Mannerist Concerns" seems a

usually start without a very clear idea of what I want... using

usually just surfaces when

TIBOR DE NAGY GALLERY

"John has a fabulous memory for arcane nonsense & not nonsense"
—Jane Freilicher to CLR, 2002

TIBOR DE NAGY GALLERY
ESTABLISHED 1950

TIBOR DE NAGY GALLERY
ESTABLISHED 1950

TIBO

4 (the unconscious)

2002, J.R.J.D.T, V-8115#

She Said, He Said

"This is visual art we're talking about, period," Ms. Spector said. "Tino made that distinction. Either you respect it or you don't. It makes perfect sense to many of us."

(Some Quality Time with the Guggenheim Museum's chief curator, Nancy Spector, courtesy of Leon Neyfakh's January 26 article in *The Observer*, "Ceci N'est Pas Performance Art.")

"According to Ms. Spector, the project is about 'finding a way to make something that is inherently ephemeral repeatable, commodifiable, collectible, preservable.'"

You enter the Guggenheim. A young hipster-ish couple lies entangled in the center of the rotunda floor, limbs and lips locked in a slo-mo pas de deux. A crowd watches from a polite distance. This is *The Kiss*.

If you stay long enough and have looked at the right artworks, you will spot the references. If you continue up the spiraling ramp, a child will rush to greet you, as if you are a present to be unwrapped. She or he will announce that you are in a piece by Tino Sehgal, invite you to follow along and ask you to define *progress*.

If you accept the invitation, you will be handed off from one conversation to another, sometimes interlocking, sometimes not. (If you say "No, thank you" and the kid in question happens to be a nonchalant little guy named Lucas, he will shrug and walk away.) *The Kiss* will continue its erotic play below. Once you reach the top and learn [spoiler alert!] that the work is titled *This Progress*, you will reverse course, return to the rotunda floor, and repeat at will.

I am a hopeless grouch.

Spector: "People are going to come in and talk about it as performance and they're going to talk about it as theater…and I feel like our job at the museum as curators and our visitor service people and even our guards is to help the public understand" that "[t]his is visual art we're talking about, period," though she conceded, according to Neyfakh, "that the distinction is a nuanced one, and is likely to bewilder many museum-goers."

"The art that matters most, Ms. Spector said, is art that changes the rules, and 'makes you consider everything that came before and what's going to come after.'"

An Email I Received from David Velasco, Artforum. com's Editor:

re *This Progress*. I'm not sure what I think. I think the most brilliant thing about his work is that he's managed to find a way to make money off of these performances (or whatever he calls them). His real innovation is in sales technique (which is no small feat, mind you). The whole thing about needing to have the interpretations passed down orally, in the presence of witnesses, with no documentation, is a bit of a coup—though it's one no other artist will be able to repeat because of how much he "owns" it. As for the work proper: I don't really like the feel-goodness of it; it seems a bit trite. But there's a cynical underbelly to it that I do sort of like—that everything is scripted, but it pretends to be profound.

"'Art sometimes just functions as an ingenious move,' Ms. Spector said. 'Richard Prince taking his first photograph of a photograph in 1977. No one else had thought of doing that at that moment. Marcel Duchamp—who else thought of the ready-made? It was sitting right there waiting to be taken…'"

The Kiss keeps going and going. Slow, controlled movement tends to be the most difficult kind for performers to sustain. Think of the way a dancer's working leg shakes as she holds a sustained balance. How beautiful it is, how much it costs her.

At least these bodies are reclining. If you've seen one choreographed kiss, have you seen them all? I'm not that interested, but I like the view from high above.

"It's hard work," says Danny, the English professor who serves as my final handler my first time up the ramp. It had taken some convincing to get him in the project at all, he adds. But he says he is having fun.

We walk very slowly. He seems to want to keep stopping. And talk about politics. I do not want to talk about politics. Always the same conversation. I give noncommittal cocktail party answers. I take notes. He doesn't ask.

When *The Kiss* is finally over, people applaud. A new kiss begins.

Spector: "I mean, funding in the visual arts is as problematic as funding in the dance world. The grass is always greener."

I remember the choreographer Layla Childs telling me at a Performa Gala back in 2008, while talk swirled of how the recession was going to impact the visual art world, that it didn't really matter to her and her colleagues, that dancers were "already living a subsistence existence."[1]

I can't remember ever seeing Nancy Spector (or any of her colleagues who are now so hot to trot for making "something that is inherently ephemeral repeatable, commodifiable, collectible, preservable") at a dance performance.

On the Ramp, an Exchange:
Julie (I think it was Julie) said she found the idea of a town designed for the good of its inhabitants creepy. (I'm not sure how we got on this topic, as she interrupted the conversation I was having with my previous handler.)
I said, that's ironic, considering.

She said, how do you mean?

I said, well, you're leading me through a designed conversation, full of things I'm supposed to talk and think about (I suspect for my own good), and your part in this is in turn thoroughly designed by Tino Sehgal.
She paused and maybe seemed uncomfortable or maybe not, and I thought perhaps something interesting was going to happen.

She said I'm not at liberty to discuss that, and changed the topic.

Progress is moving forward but not knowing if you're going in the right direction. Like Oppenheimer.

Some Things I Have Read About Tino Sehgal, and *This Progress*:

99

"What fascinates me about Sehgal is that working only with human clay, he can call forth thoughtful and visceral responses from people who remain unmoved by more conventional paintings and sculptures. ... If you regard Sehgal as a twenty-first-century sculptor who abjures digging stone out of a ravaged earth, then the interviews that he conducted of grade-school children and teenage college students throughout the city were the ecologically informed equivalent of the scouting missions that Michelangelo made to the marble quarries of Carrara."[2]

The sweet-faced teenage boy walking beside me wonders who Oppenheimer was.

"The fact that Sehgal's works are produced in this way elicits a different kind of viewer: a visitor is no longer only a passive spectator, but one who bears a responsibility to shape and at times to even contribute to the actual realization of the piece. The work may ask visitors what they think, but, more importantly, it underscores an individual's own agency in the museum environment. Regardless of whether they call for direct action or address the viewer in a more subtle sense, Sehgal's works always evoke questions of responsibility within an interpersonal relationship."[3]

I suppose it isn't ideal to enter a show full of preconceived notions. But it sure is fun.

"You will enjoy your visit to the Tino Sehgal whatchamacallit at the Guggenheim—"show" doesn't fill the bill—or else expose yourself as a hopeless grouch."[4]

Sehgal strictly controls any sort of documentation about the work itself (he apparently gets pretty hot under the collar about the now ubiquitous leaking of cell phone photos.)[5]

Some Other Things Said to Me by Tino Sehgal's Human Clay:

"Tino's quite fussy about the title." "I guess once you get used to cutting-edge art it's not so strange." "Keep talking, you have to keep talking." "Is that a serious proposition?" "It's not performance. I'm making art!" "You were so intent on dissecting the piece, the piece couldn't happen." "Not the money we get, which is just at the very edge of real." (After I joked that everything about the piece is conceptual "except the money.")

There's a difference between interesting and clever.

A Text Message I Received About *This Progress*:
"Oh no!! I loved it. I somewhat resent that there is a narrowly-cast objective masquerading a bit as a free-form inquiry but I find the topic so agreeable that I don't mind!! Overall I think it's very stimulating and spatially transformative—the art is in the people instead of on the walls. I like that."

One Last Thing Said to Me by the Human Clay:
"There's no artwork on the walls to distract you."

It's true. I lie in one of the vacant white stalls and think of Simone Forti's dance constructions and the whole Judson Dance Theater conversation about minimalist dance and sculpture. Of Jérôme Bel. Of 101 site-specific performances, good, bad, and ugly. Of Fluxus and Chris Burden. Of Miguel Gutierrez's 2001 durational work *Freedom of Information*, in which he moved continuously for 24 hours, his eyes covered and his ears plugged.

I think of Holland Cotter's review of Sehgal, how energized *This Progress* made him. How the only thing all these dissatisfying conservations had in common was me, and how passive my participation had seemed. Like being part of a live wall text.

I think of the last time I was this desperate to flee the Guggenheim, during Performa 2007, at the Italian artist Francesco Vezzoli's celebrity-jammed production of the 1917 Pirandello play *Right You Are (If You Think You Are)*. Such a smug, airless affair. How good it felt to walk out into the dark city air.

The smallest bits of Human Clay lean against some planted grasses[6] at the bottom of the ramp, joking and whispering and touching each others' heads while making sizzling "sssss" sounds and altogether having the best conversations of the day.[7]

If you opted out of *This Progress* you could opt instead to take an audio tour up the ramp, and learn all about the museum's architecture. Either way, you had to exit through the gift shop. The cashier had "no idea" why the exit was rerouted thusly. She seemed rather put out at being asked.

Geography
for B.

Well, that's how I feel.
        I'd like to be
  Norway, land
of A-frames
                            Land
of the midnight sun
        all over the horizon, the water
    spilling out
like cod liver oil
billions of silver-scaled fish swarming to get in, get out; no-
        body wants
to be landlocked. Nobody wants to be
                        Switzerland.
It just happens.

The Missing World
for Tom

I've gotten deep into it, to the spaceship phase, to the
center of the universe.
The problem is, I'm always in love with at least three people
I am now building a long, slow campaign to colonize
different galaxies.

Minerva ties golden threads around her neck and steps
into the streets.
Ruined woodwork and ghosts
The fountain is dry.
The iron girls swing onto their horses.
The olive trees shake their silver bellies at the stars.
Minerva becomes an owl.
The water towers become spaceships, the olive trees
shed their bellies.
The satellites aren't in the mood for uninvited guests.
That's the trouble with tribesmen, the Uzbek warlord
thinks to himself: too busy stealing each other's ponies
to think ahead.

Minerva makes her way around an endless rim.
Seaweed slaps against the seawall.
The god sleeps in his copper running shoes.
Every year the bearded lady grows less manageable, less
swayed by coinage.
There are complaints.
The walkways through the empty courtyard are never
short enough.

Again the Visigoths steal the Uzbek warlord's favorite pony.
My heart is enlarged, Minerva whispers, it is breaking.

Another skyline in the other ancient city
The local girls toy with their life savings, wait for a
different salesman to arrive.

The gypsies are too feckless, the Uzbek warlord
decides, to be counted on if and when he launches the
Caspian Sea invasion.
The evening widens over Minerva, pooling in her alien
heart face.
Scramble headstone lingerie bricks.
The hill peacocks scream, just beyond the outer walls.
The chosen hero beats the drums
The meat trembles in its aluminum packing crate, five
miles out from the processing plant.

Now you are in the sandbox
You can kill a man any way you choose, walk in any direction.
This weather, so exchangeable
Lacquered shutters close against midday heat.
A row of cypress trees
A girl running barefoot, nightgown a white balloon, the
sea a strip of worked metal.
I chase a child superhero through the jungles of an
unknown planet, eat him on the plains.

The mind agitates
Another fine mess begins to take delicate shape before
the Uzbek warlord's weary eyes.
Minerva thinks a long time about what to do.
She practices fierce, deadly karate kicks.
Are You Looking for Adventure? Want to Fight for Riches?
So far, no one has answered the Uzbek warlord's ad;
maybe, he thinks, he will try the dailies.
Probably, he thinks, yes he is almost sure, that was
where things had gone really wrong.

It takes the god a long time to get over the nonbelievers.
He spends long hours in the cafeteria, arranging the
mixed vegetables by color
Minerva turns again to the stacked cardboard
mountains: such strangeness in her terrible eyes.
The open window, he is waiting
The molecular cloning men come at night in their
white suits, sometimes carrying snacks.
The pigeon eyes the god nervously, there, twisting on
the AstroTurf in his absurdly clean tennis shoes.

Finally, the god demands payment for making the
world more interesting.
He buys the bomb that will blow up time
The citizenry is not pleased with this development.
Minerva wishes for the mountain to explode and take
some of her sisters with it.
Eventually, everyone reaches the hardest setting

Still, some days (or nights—who could tell up here?)
the Uzbek warlord misses his old pony, Stendhal, who
would surely have liked seeing the stars.

we want do the actual stapling ⑥
i'll just say... stapling

The secretaries are not cold

one other thing
our man - he can't stand up by himself yet

So if starts w/ the footnote
do you need to see that
I need to see everything
lets do pause & then lets freeze

Somebody's always getting just what she wants
bodies that don't work
bodies that are more than bodies
the whore is always alone
You may never be heroic
they strike poses
they disgust us, themselves
wood like flesh
pause
secret messages
I forget how to take notes
I don't notice the right things
you find comfort in being alone

107

Taste

It's not always easy to look at things

Well, it's easy to look at war. Think about traffic accidents.

The concrete horizon

The white room

Don't worry, man, the black won't rub off on you

All that bubble gum awfulness pink

All the little boys parading around

Look at you

Your implants are perfect I tried to hibernate in them

I don't know what I'm doing here

I'm just so....oh. I don't know

Getting naked is for amateurs.

This is not an official no

Those people come down here, they don't contribute anything

They talk about the quality of the light

The all new & improved

Don't worry, the black won't

These two are real professionals.

They're very flexible.

Something about that white flower, that dark hair

I saw my first hooker in Miami

Stick insect orange street lights stretch

It's like they say, you only know what gunshots sound
like after you hear one

They don't look like anything else

It's really beautiful

It's really good

It's easy to look at war. Think about traffic accidents.

Those people come down here

They talk about the quality of the light

Payment options

High-rise

Lowrider

Euphoria spelled wrong

Don't worry,

That one's white as milk

Right now they're taking pictures

Don't be so cynical darling Bend over

The way the palm fronds suck their teeth

The wrongest images repeat

I've got a caseload of these See? I resort to couplets

I rhyme. I take notes. I retreat.

You know I could just keep generating

The stray dogs are running through the streets

The stars are all over you

The lovers, after work, must wash each other's feet

These two are very flexible.

They're real professionals.

In the dream I am dressed like them.

I'm just so…

The all new & improved

It only matters if you charge money

The taste of metal against your teeth

I mean it's not always easy to look

This is my job and I can tell you it's not always easy

I mean, I never give money to the homeless

I'm not that kind of humanitarian

I just like it when you do that I like it when you do it just like that

The body works it out

The body gets closer

Standing in the sun squinting

Of course we're all mourning for ourselves

Of course we get uncomfortable around our kind

It's subjective

But look at that torso

The way his pelvis slides into his thigh

Goddamn technology

What. Are you going to take a picture now?

To put it more bluntly: do you even know what you're doing here?

High-rise Lowrider

The black won't rub off

This outfit wasn't my idea

I like that because it's shiny I like you because I don't
have to think

I packed for the end of the world

What? I'm a professional watcher

The black won't rub off on you

The girls won't come this way again

I mean, just look at them

That one likes to spend money

I mean, just look at him

He wraps himself in gold just because it's Tuesday

These two are perfect. Their bodies are wrecked; they
are doing that for us

We come down here, we don't contribute anything

We talk about the quality of the light

Isn't that something Cherry Coke remarkable isn't that…

You make sense without words

The frigate birds wheel high above, sharpening their knives

I do not want to spend my life without knowing anything else

We look at war

We look at the crushed flowers from the night before

The carpet is impossibly white

The tower is a double crescent

Rubber doll, techno something

You've never met more awkward rock stars

There is a way in which the translator must love failure

The thin line of light splitting the morning sky

Map for PG

South Central Soviet Union, page 28

As if you were fucking him
As if she were the last girl on earth
As if we were otherwise unentertainable

China, Mongolia, page 31

The boys and their ponies
Minerva crying on the red ropey rug
Homesick

Central and Southern Argentina and Chile, page 54

It's two hours ahead there
No it's four, six
Pick up Styx
I wanted my blood on your hand
Where I'd pressed against you
What's another word for derelict?

Eastern Brazil, page 57

Darling.
Love.
You never ate my enemies the way I asked you to
I filled my veins with glue

Once Upon a Time

"The problem with science is all facts are manipulated."

The woman was talking to her friend in Kaffismiðja Íslands, a small, homespun café in Reykjavik. Good lattes and buttery croissants. The woman was Scottish, I think. Let's just say definitely, and she was making a point about Margaret Thatcher—speaking ill of the dead, though respectfully, if one can be said to speak ill of the dead respectfully.

The problem with science is the pleasure with art.

This year's Sequences VI, a "real-time art festival," was ten days long, a day for every year that Gretar Reynisson, the festival's honorary artist, spent making his durational collection *Decade*. I spent five of those days at the festival, wandering, mostly alone, through the quiet streets of a city with only about 120,000 inhabitants. Most places you look there is the chalky white of the mountains or the midnight blue of the ocean—there aren't so many trees, and the ones that do exist are surprisingly delicate, in that northern stunted way. (What do you do if you're lost in the forest? asks the Icelandic joke. Stand up.)

Reynisson's *Decade* began January 1, 2001, and ended December 31, 2010. During this time he worked toward no exhibitions, but rather collected the material and detritus of the everyday: pillows, drinking glasses, white dress shirts. "Some people call this an obsession, but nevertheless..." the artist explains in a slender catalog. "I like creating rules."

It's a romantic idea, at once egomaniacal and Sisyphean: ten years to assemble something that most people will wander through in well under ten minutes. But then, Sequences VI is a romantic festival. "I was very much thirsty for a new approach, something nonacademic," said its curator, Markús Þór Andrésson. I think he was after something thoughtful and theatrical, a festival that wears its heart on its sleeve, only the sleeve is removable. "If we can all just accept this old-fashioned idea of theater, of doing something fake, then something true can happen as well."

And let's face it, Iceland is a romantic place, at least for a visitor. True, the locals are worn out with reading foreign press accounts of their remote island utopia. But what are writers without our lazy framing devices? The impulse behind this one is immensely understandable: When you're on a chunk of volcanic rock in the middle of the Atlantic, slipping from gallery to geothermic hot spring to bar and back again, you're maybe in the mood to be seduced.

Here's one hopelessly romantic item: Hotel Holt, where most of the Sequences guests seemed to be staying, houses the largest privately owned art collection in Iceland. None of the usual horrific hotel wall decorations—the place is packed with quality works, and in fact it's the closest thing the city has to a permanent public display, since the museum doesn't have one.

"Growing up in Iceland, you never see the art object, you never see art history," said Ragnar Kjartansson, who these days is working pretty much everywhere.

"It's very hard, if you grow up in this environment, to understand art as an object. It's also quite good; there's no burden of history."

But of course there's always history. Kjartansson's contribution to Sequences is a set of small self-portraits, the lone figure rather ghostly amid the Easter Egg colors of the room—a room in Hotel Holt, where Kjartansson checked in, ordered room service, and settled in to paint. "Holt was the temple, the only place to see real art," he said. "So this was a total homage."

For the duration of the festival, at least, Kjartansson is in the temple, his paintings tucked amid the modernist abstractions and rugged seascapes that contemporary artists are now saddled with. "You can't show beautiful landscapes and be serious about it, not here," said Ragnheiður Gestsdóttir, whose quiet installation at the Reykjavik Sculpture Association manipulates the facts of landscape by placing a little cutout man in the center of an image of a natural amphitheater—ground zero for the shifting tectonic plates of Europe and North America, and also where Iceland's parliament used to meet, back when they were Vikings. He's holding it all together; she's having her cake and eating it too. History.

Several other rooms at Hotel Holt had been taken over by Sequences, including Room 206, where Hans Rosenström's sound piece *Blindsight* was holed up, waiting to whisper, in Icelandic, to an audience of one. Who knows what the neighboring guests made of the traffic in and out at all hours. With any luck, Holt will get a reputation for being one of *those* hotels.

On Saturday night, Holt was overflowing, playing host to an evening of Sequences performance art. The thing with site-specific shows, you have to be a nimble audience member or you're stuck staring at the backs of taller people's heads. I kept returning to a durational piece by Magnús Logi Kristinsson, which at first blush struck me as eye-rollingly tedious. Great. Another artist in a box; if I'd wanted this I'd have stayed home and gawked at Tilda.

Only you couldn't gawk here, you could only see Kristinsson's left leg and right arm, both extended from the white rectangular box. Someone untied his black dress shoe; someone retied it. People took photographs and giggled, etc. As the veins in his hand began to bulge, my jaded mood shifted. The things people do! I gave his anonymous arm a quick massage, feeling shy and bold at the same time.

This was shortly after, or maybe before, critic Oliver Basciano said to me: "You feel like a cynical bastard. But then that's our job." We both held drinks, as I remember. We both laughed. He was talking about his experience of watching Guido van der Werve's film *Nummer veertien, home* at artist-run space Kling & Bang Gallery, which weaves together the everyday business of living with the idea of the epic quest: Van der Werve traveled, triathlon-style, from Frédéric Chopin's birthplace in Warsaw to his grave in Paris, his own personal campaign to keep going.

Basciano was talking, I think, about having to write what exists beyond the pleasing surface. Not to be romanced. I understand what he means, and also I'm not so sure. Is it possible to fail through resistance? "This whole horrible period of postmodernism has created this line," Andrésson had said earlier, with a weary laugh. "Everything must be taken with a distance, with skepticism. It's very difficult to unlearn this, when a whole generation of artists and audiences has been through this."

One of the sections in van der Werve's film is titled *Please Be Safe*. On Monday, amid news of the bombings in Boston, I remembered that he had been planning to run the marathon. I was happy to hear that he made it through ok.

More this, less that
after Anna Sperber

Veins in the hand   Foot six
inches off the ground

Sweat pooling   Leather fringe

                        You will run You will run

These are the only dragons

                  Black checker board like brushed
satin nickel

            [Of if not, why not][1]

This idea of smallness and bigness all at once "What
are you doing what" Romeo will never come Juliet finds
other diversions   She still dies young

The pipes are shaking
                  The scaffolding is backlit
                                    Lunge lunge
The longer I do this the worse I get at it

I can put my leg here

                  It's not important
I am the elegant blonde   Everything is whistling

Miles Davis in Spain   We begin again & again & again
        Speed The will to power

Persephone, and what came after
The sight of the encounter   The jaw resolves
Puncture wound
Our politics change, not our emotions

                         Or is it the other way around?
We end up waiting   Our taped feet darken like
chimney sweeps
If we could rise up now and float over you

          [If not, then why not]

Oh right   The street lights outside   The cracked bowl
Porcelain   Filament   Aftermath

The jet roars overhead.

her arms rise & the lights seem to go up
they give instructions
she ignores
I dont help
K is always hunted, haunted
how you can feel shy
I don't know what they're doing
they don't know what they're doing
I like the tableaux... the pietà...
a dance for actors
how you can use the outrageous to hide in
  plain sight. it never really works. not
in the long run
their bodies more tragic. lunges. flat backs

And Then With Bodies

I suppose you could call Ralph Lemon an interdisciplinary artist. But somehow the term seems flat and cumbersome in describing his output, which at this point feels more like a continuing set of questions and proposals than a series of distinct pieces. He is building a body of work in the truest sense, reaching for a poetics at once complex and simple and constructing a container to receive, if only for scattered moments, things that can't be kept.

For those familiar with his performances and visual art, the New York premiere of *How Can You Stay in the House All Day and Not Go Anywhere?* on Wednesday at the Brooklyn Academy of Music was replete with intimate resonances. For those not, Mr. Lemon began the evening with a primer of sorts: *Sunshine Room*, a film (edited by Mike Taylor) surveying some of his key themes and collaborators and looking back at his large stage production *Come Home Charley Patton* (2004).

Mr. Lemon tucked his thin, supple body into a white chair onstage, just in front of a large screen, a thin sheaf of papers on his lap and a microphone before him; it was as if we were settling down for story time. Chief among his collaborators in recent years has been Walter Carter, a former sharecropper born in 1908. And there Mr. Carter was on the screen, on his Mississippi property, clambering into a homespun spaceship that looked as if it wouldn't get him to the market, much less the moon: life, art and artifice, all improbably tangled up.

"This is Walter, my teacher," a recording of Mr. Lemon's voice informed us. "This is one of my lessons."

With Mr. Carter, who died this year, Mr. Lemon built a layered world of fable, political archetypes and the everyday. The older man seemed at times to serve as the artist's avatar, helping Mr. Lemon get at things that were too much for him to touch on his own. In *Sunshine Room*, one of these is the demise of Asako Takami, Mr. Lemon's partner, who died in 2007 after a long illness; *How Can You Stay* is dedicated to her and Mr. Carter, as well as to Merce Cunningham and Pina Bausch. The losses stack up and up and up.

"After three and a half years of denying it could ever happen, it took Asako only 18 hours to disappear," Mr. Lemon told us. She is never in the film. Instead there are Mr. Carter and his wife, Edna, reenacting scenes from the original *Solaris* (1972), the Tarkovsky science-fiction movie in which a man is visited by his dead wife in outer space. They are at once themselves, the film characters, Mr. Lemon and Ms. Takami, and none of the above.

The quiet, meditative elegy of this first section gave way to Part 2, *Wall/hole*, a go-for-broke dance performed by Mr. Lemon's six enthralling performers (who helped create the material) that picks up on the end movement of *Charley Patton*. Dressed in colorful slacks and shirts, the dancers hurled themselves through space, legs buckling, joints smacking the floor, torsos unfurling like ribbons in the wind. They seemed boneless at times, their bodies collapsing into dense scrums, then scattering. It was painful to watch, sometimes exhilarating, sometimes only wearying: a physical overdose coming hard on the heels of a delicate grappling with grief, love, and theater. Okwui Okpokwasili, the performer perhaps most associated with Mr. Lemon, whipped herself in circles with one arm flung out, seemingly in an ecstatic trance. Later, after the stage had cleared of its chaotic bodies and the audience sat in semidarkness, her wailing cries filled the theater.

She eventually edged onto the stage, her bare back to us, shuddering and heaving and, finally, just before exiting again, almost casually picking up a tambourine. Given Mr. Lemon's exploration of racial stereotypes and expectations, it was hard not to think of black American artists who have performed facing away from the audience, refusing the role of entertainer even as they entertained.

Another potent and fraught figure often conjured by Mr. Lemon, Brer Rabbit, reappeared in a video designed by Jim Findlay. He was surrounded by a gathering of animals, rendered in ghostly white outlines, which ambled onto the dark backdrop. The audience stared at them. They stared back.

I thought of two lines from *Sunshine Room*, which came after Mr. Carter had asked the hare the question for which the overall work is titled: "The hare stares blankly. The question is, of course, the answer and the form in which the answer exists."

Mr. Lemon asks so many questions, in so many forms. (*How Can You Stay* continues with *Meditation*, a free film installation at the Kitchen on Sunday.) His answers, at some level, always seem to contain a "yes." And this was the last word he uttered onstage on Wednesday, after he and Ms. Okpokwasili had cycled through *No Room*, a subdued duet that read like an echo of the earlier kinetic free-for-all (and was lighted with painterly remove by Roderick Murray).

Mr. Lemon said it as a matter of fact, an answer that was also another question. Yes. What else could he have said? Life and art go on, until they don't.

RESERVED

RESERVED

Unintentional Relationships

I had been traveling for hours, not quite 24 hours, to arrive in this little nowhere city, covered in a sky full of action. I changed my money and found the train station.

I don't know how to end things, and also how responsible I am.

The possibility which theater provides to try to do something about faith.

I hate needless complexity, Nancy says. I love complexity, though.

I can't say anything useful in your language.

I waited and waited to do this and then I lost my window and then I did it anyway and now I am not sure.

I like art that's useful to be around.

All these corporate logos in the back of a book that tells us this event is not logo-centric, does not believe in the inevitable zoom of electronic growth.

Then I saw Jesus on the mountain.

Art as salve for loneliness.

To be mortal in the immortal moment.
I am eating one of the vegetable samosas the Indian

woman sells in her shop for 1 euro.

"But the real heart of Berlin is a small damp black wood—the Tiergarten."

Not to stop ourselves, not to have expectations, rules.

The midlife crisis begins to become understandable.

Right onto Museumplatz.

I have to have it and no I don't want it.

All the buildings like wedding cakes, all the widows like buildings.

If you want quiet, kill them all.

In the dream he tells me about the new girlfriend.

My skull aches & I have to pee & I am oppressed by my body's need to die—its need, in other words, to be a body.

Don't you feel any relationship between writing and movement?

The body sinking down, only thinking to be at rest, until it is.

Endless information on the fire hydrant.

How beautiful hands and feet are.

"I feel bad."

I lose my concentration.

Maybe you want to become this person who puts the cards out and not only grins and seethes.

It's not all to pretend you don't know, but to be present for what you know already.

This vulnerability & desire for something enigmatic and self-contained.

It's possible I spend too much time in theaters.
Always the arms linked.

Always the airplanes rushing by.

Fable

When she grew very old the Medusa decided to give her true heart away. It was, of course, made of stone. She was, again, very old, and unlovely, though not in an unhandsome way.

She saved up her courage to ask the Moon if she might come for a visit, and clear her head. "This country," she wrote, "this country is a disaster. The gay bars play the History Channel. Stream of consciousness turns out to be a gutter."

She packed light (other than her heart). She had no particular needs. Only to find a Star Man, to explain to him The Desperate Scene.

The Moon was put out, and shrank to a sliver. The Medusa drank ouzo, and signed for all deliveries. She turned a few satellites to stone, but her heart—forgive the pun—wasn't in it.

No suitable Star Men came. The Medusa decided to die. She found an asteroid for a grave. She gave her heart to the Moon before leaving. The Moon, typically, did not know whether to be irritated, or relieved. They said their goodbyes. Shortly thereafter, the Moon contracted an incurable disease.

She Stands on Your Head

Places the whole world on it
No it's a palm frond
Cuts her finger
One dried small stick in and out
The black sand is not really black
The black oystercatchers aren't either
Their vermilion beaks like something not of this world
Nor the one on your head
Yes she really did do that
Fingers typing wildly
Trying to position the layers of sediment
This isn't it this isn't it you think wildly
But her great eyeless eyes are already sweeping over you
and up
The evening widens then shrinks
The big twisted trunk breaks loose
Over the red roofs and the satin party dresses laid out
to dry
Everywhere an extravagance except where you need it
Everywhere a way of becoming that is sure to wound
you badly
You open your mouth
The water streams in, streams out
The sad woman flips a switch
And again this world heavy on you
No it fell
It wasn't made for staying you say you say
The others listen, are quiet
The whole damn thing takes up too much space
And so that's it
Your mouth closes into an untidy fist

No darlings you tell them and they listen but not quietly
The moon is tender *ce soir*, he says with his funny accent
You laugh all the way home
But you do not make a sound.

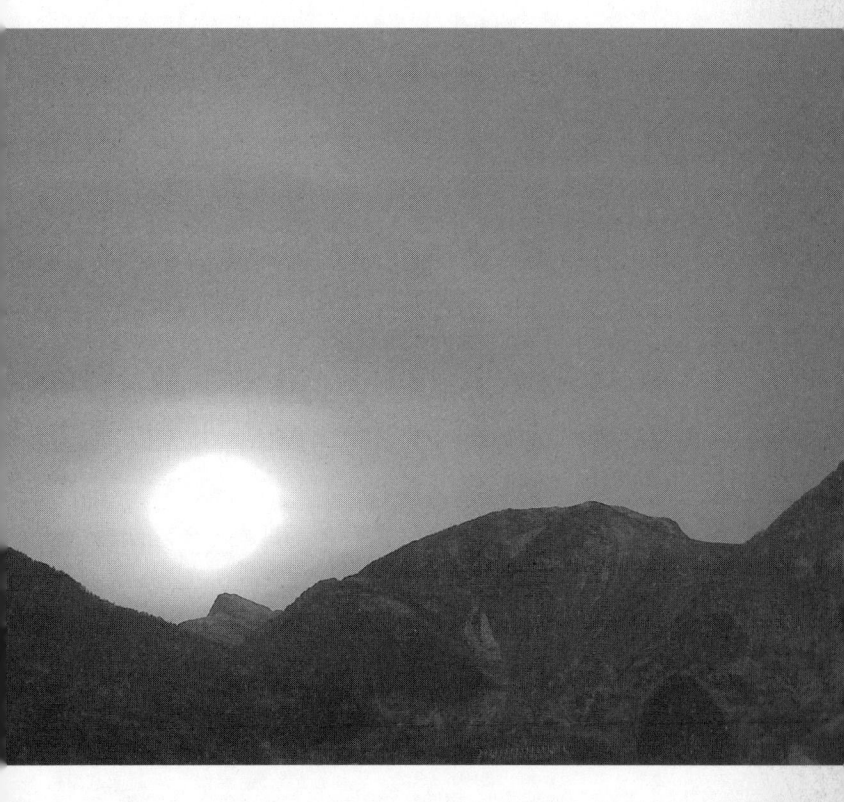

A Merce Cunningham Dance Company Quickie (with an extended Trisha Brown Parenthetical)

Brandon Collwes, Dylan Crossman, Julie Cunningham, Emma Desjardins, Jennifer Goggans, John Hinrichs, Daniel Madoff, Rashaun Mitchell, Marcie Munnerlyn, Krista Nelson, Silas Riener, Jamie Scott, Robert Swinston, Melissa Toogood, Andrea Weber: those are all of them, the very last of the Mohicans.

Come New Year's Eve, it will all be over. What an impossible thing to consider—until you think of what the alternative might be (a calcified object limping along, with no thought of why or how)—and then you're filled with gratitude, that somebody had the guts to do the right thing, pull the plug while the heart was still beating. We don't last. Why do we think art has to?

(I also thought about this while watching the Trisha Brown Dance Company, performing just down 19th Street at Dance Theater Workshop, the same too-cold-for-spring weeks in late March. Brown's glory years began in the 1960s and I think maybe ebbed out in the early '90s, a brilliant 30-plus year rush—how fiercely you sense the intensely sophisticated and playful mind driving that work, and how strange and sad and beautiful it is to see her now, so frail, as Cunningham was toward the end, but different, to see her lost in that work, and held by it, hair rumpled and a little girl smile on her face as she bows with her dancers, who are so gentle with her, and so breakneck with themselves. It's their turn.)

Why do we even want it to last? What is that all about? So we can engage in the same endless, awful, predictable debate about whether such-and-such a dance was better 30 years ago, how so-and-so dancers just don't get what the work should be? (Like who the hell are we to say that shit and think it means *anything*?)

The last Sunday afternoon in March was the last *CRWDSPCR* ever. I don't know what it looked like at the premiere in 1993. I wasn't there. On Sunday it was glorious beyond glorious, the dancers pushing through exhaustion to meet the choreography's impossible demands, and—this was the real kicker—smiling as they did it, not those stupid presentational facsimiles people sometimes slap on, but smiling—*laughing*, really—to themselves and each other as they went about their business. Ordinary. Exalted. Netted in John King's marvelous sounds. They didn't have to be anything other than themselves, and neither did we, and I felt lucky to be in just this place on just this day.

It wasn't the definitive version of *CRWDSPCR*. Just the final one, and only for those who saw it, and even then maybe it was several somebody's first one, too. Outside, the sky was a perfect distant blue, a color that my friend said did not exist, unless it was maybe "aching blue."

He was smoking a cigarette and I think eating potato chips. We watched as one of the dancers, finished for the day, hurried from the Joyce Theater, movie star incognito in dark sunglasses. We were sentimental; he had places to be.

There were these things

You'd call them clouds
You'd call me conventional

Darling darling darling

I had this idea of all things coming together
That there would be time
And no time

Like you say, practicing
The man next to me is beautiful
He looks out the window

There are these things
You'd call them clouds
You'd call me conventional

I don't anymore want to call you darling
The problem is one of attention span
The problem is one of the problems

I found a bunker for the bodies
I found a

It's true what they say
I'm already repeating myself the loop isn't that big
The chemical continues to claim its flesh

There could be these things
There are are these things

I even want the mistakes maybe that's all I want
Maybe I want the man next to me but that isn't practical

The woman can't miss her flight she stresses this
information this fact
We don't we don't we don't care do we my ex-darling
sometimes maybe darling again

Shot down again
The president makes his funny face he doesn't like we
disagree with him

Oh oh oh
I justify left you justify right no one claims the center
It feels like hell
There is blue thinly being blue
There is white

The old man cuts in line and this is why we don't like
old men
Also they're not useful

But you see there would have been, at one point, as it
were, these *things*
And then everyone would've been sunglasses wiped
clean

Darling
No.
Nothing in nothing out
The system finally wants to be locked

The system, finally, wants to be wants

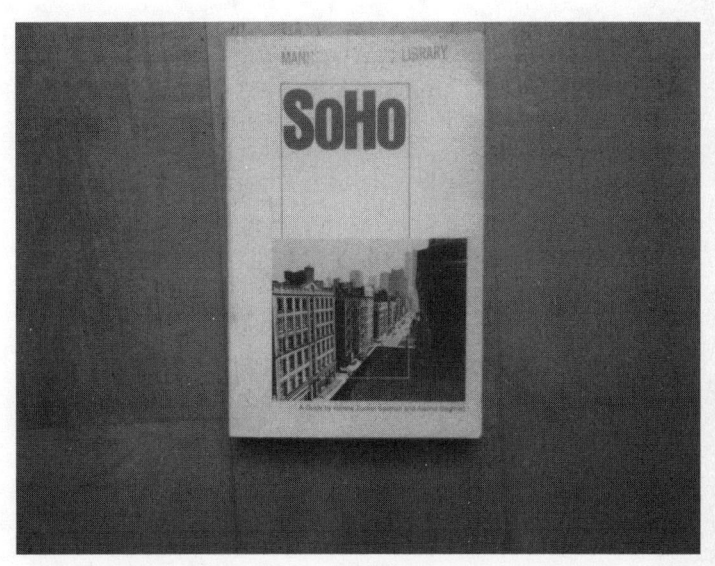

The bad cat came but I chased him away
for Kate

Always & ever thus
Mangy cat ass
I can see you poking around my weeds

Get outta here, goddamn cat
like there won't be a tomorrow
like this is the thing I'll be doing my whole lousy life

It's hot
Will I be ready in a little while?
Will I be able to adjust?
How long can a person recover before it becomes
another form of not being?

I love you, though, cat.
It's a new form of uncertainty

Take the best most useless dress and tie it on your head
Maybe then the real bad cat will really drop dead

I'm going into that canyon
And you shall not know me when I return
Not all of me
Not yet

NOTES

Just go for it, go for it

1. Cynthia Carr, *The Life and Times of David Wojnarowicz* (New York: Bloomsbury USA, 2012), 536.
2. Elizabeth Bishop, "One Art," in *The Complete Poems*, (New York: The Noonday Press, 1983), 178.
3. Tom Ford, "Lucho and Juliet," *CR Fashion Book*, no. 1.

On Taste

1. An email Silas and Rashaun sent to me, Davison and James Kidd on January 9th, 2013.
2. Ibid. [At first I typed ibis, a happy error.]
3. He has been described as charismatic, animalistic. Silas, who is of (black?) Irish descent, is much more animalistic as a dancer, I would say; I'm not sure if he has ever been described that way. This makes me think of Serena and Venus Williams, how their success is often described in terms of sheer, brute physicality, while their (almost always white) opponents are more likely to be discussed in terms of strategy. And then I think (especially when in Florida) of Indian Wells, the inevitable annual calls for the Williams sisters to return. Really? What's in that for them?
4. R. talking to me during dinner at Pangea, a restaurant across the street from Danspace Project, in New York, where the next iteration of *Taste* was performed in November 2013.
5. This is true.
6. Actually, I'm not sure if that's better, or worse. "At least" might be misleading here.

She said, He said

1. "Future Imperfect," Claudia La Rocco, Artforum.com, November 23, 2008.
2. "Making Art Out of an Encounter," Arthur Lubow, *New York Times Magazine*, January 15, 2010.
3. Tino Sehgal's exhibit at the Guggenheim.
4. "Never-Ending Story," Peter Schjeldahl, *The New Yorker*, February 15, 2010.
5. Art world drama! Tino Sehgal calls the *New York Times* "crass."
6. Judging by the dying vegetative evidence scattered around their feet, they appear to pass the time in part by pulling out said vegetation.

CREDITS

The author is grateful for permission to reprint from the following artists and publishers: "They Always Ask for Water" on Hyperallergic.com, January 21, 2012; "White Waves, Dark Cliffs" from *The New York Times*, June 12, 2009 © 2009 *The New York Times*; "Forget About Your Paper Moon" from *The New York Times*, January 13, 2012 © 2012 *The New York Times*; "Hinge and Straighten" from *The New York Times*, May 6, 2011 © 2011 *The New York Times*; "Love or Money" on Artforum.com, May 26, 2013; "Leisurely Promenade" on ThePerformanceClub.org, May 7, 2013; "Everyday People" on Artforum.com, February 8, 2013; "*Space//Space* Stream of Consciousness" on ThePerformanceClub.org, June 15, 2012; "On Taste" in the *Miami Rail*, Summer 2013; "Once Upon a Time" on Artforum.com, May 7, 2013; "And Then With Bodies" from *The New York Times*, October 15, 2010 © 2010 *The New York Times*; "More this, less that" on ThePerformanceClub.org, May 3, 2013; "Unintentional Relationships" on ThePerformanceClub.org, Sept 20, 2012; "John Ashbery: 'Collages: They Knew What They Wanted'" in *The Brooklyn Rail*, October 10, 2008; "She Said, He Said" in *The Brooklyn Rail*, March 4, 2010; "Geography" on failbetter.com, August 8, 2007; "Taste" on ThePerformanceClub.org, April 11, 2013; "A Merce Cunningham Dance Company Quickie" in *The Brooklyn Rail*, April 5, 2011.

"Taste" was written and performed as part of Rashaun Mitchell and Silas Riener's *Taste*, a site-specific performance and installation presented at the BFI Gallery in Miami, in partnership with O, Miami. April 2013.

"173-177 [or: Facebook Is Inescapable]" was written (after reading five pages of Edward Said) as a site-specific piece for the wall of José Carlos Teixeira's studio as part of his *Translation(s)*, a project developed at Headlands Center for the Arts. July 2013.

"Just go for it, go for it" was developed during the creation of *Biograph, last year was pretty/shitty* (January 2013, Oslo, Norway), by the Norway-based interdisciplinary performance company Findlay//Sandsmark.

"Map for PG" was written as source material for *Quartet* (2013) by the composer Phillip Greenlief.

The handwritten "Notes" were made in conversation with an in-progress dance by the choreographer Karen Sherman, performed by Joanna Furnans, Jeffrey Wells and Karen Sherman during a residency at the Vermont Performance Lab. September 2012.

ABOUT THE AUTHOR

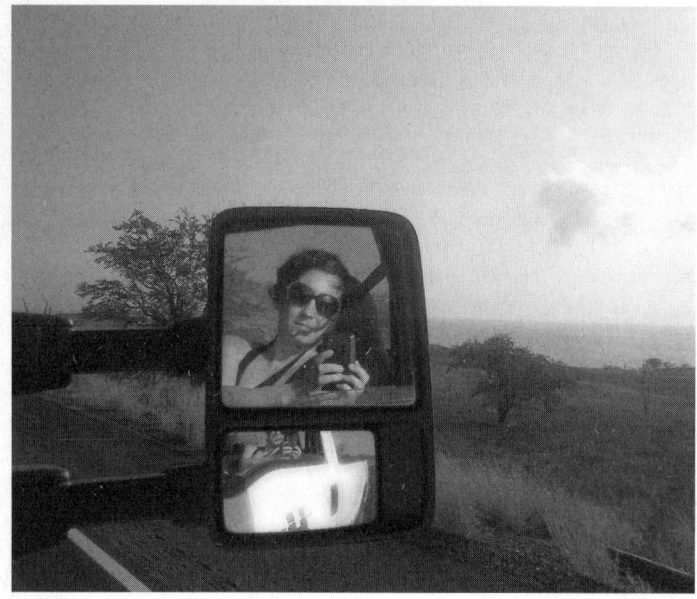

Claudia La Rocco is a writer, teacher and performer whose work often revolves around interdisciplinary collaboration. She lives in Brooklyn.